Passing the
Risk Management Professional
(PMI-RMP)® Certification Exam
the First Time!

Second Edition

Daniel C. Yeomans, MBA, PMI-RMP, PMI-PMP,
PMI-ACP, CSM, CMQ/OE

This edition published by
Dog Ear Publishing
4010 W. 86th Street, Ste H
Indianapolis, IN 46268

www.dogearpublishing.net

ISBN: 978-145750-018-3
This book is printed on acid-free paper.

Printed in the United States of America

Passing the Risk Management Professional (PMI-RMP)® Certification Exam the First Time!

Second Edition

<u>Author:</u> Daniel C. Yeomans, PMI-RMP, PMI-PMP, PMI-ACP, CSM, CMQ/OE

<u>Editors:</u> Patricia Carey, PMP, and Rob Childress

<u>Acknowledgements in Alphabetical Order:</u>

Patricia Carey, PMP

Cynthia Holmberg, PMP

Peter Rogers, MBA

Gilmere Vieira, PMP

The first edition of this book was dedicated to all my friends and associates at Northwest University and Microsoft Corporation who provided valued input, ideas, and support.

I also dedicated that edition to my youngest daughter, Erika, who serenaded me with lovely piano and flute music while I worked.

This second edition is dedicated to all who purchased the first edition and passed the PMI-RMP®—and along the way, urged me to update the book to reflect changes in the test. For all you do, this edition is for you!

Table of Contents

Preface

Project Risk Management is a challenging area of project management that can make or break a project. It is often said that project risk will find you, if you do not find it first. This book uses a six-step approach to risk that was developed by the Project Management Institute (PMI)®. This approach follows the proven Plan-Do-Check-Act, or PDCA, methodology developed many years ago by W. Edwards Deming and Walter A. Shewhart[1]. Step one to effectively manage risk is to *Plan* effectively. Once you develop a plan, follow it, or *Do* it. *Check* to ensure the plan is working and *Act* accordingly, based on your findings.

The PMI Risk Management Professional (PMI-RMP®) certification was introduced in 2008. This certification acknowledges the continuing pressure to complete projects on time, within budget, and provide the scope needed by the customer. Per PMI, "Qualified Risk Management Professionals are needed on project management teams. The Project Management Institute recognizes the importance and special qualifications needed to be a Project Risk Management Professional. The PMI-RMP credential will substantiate the applicant's knowledge, skills and experience in this area.[2]"

This book is designed for Project Managers and other professionals who may or may not want to attain the PMI-RMP certification. It takes you through the journey of a proven Risk Management Process and includes activities and practice test questions that will help you achieve the goal of passing the certification examination the first time. In addition, I am confident that your individual abilities to plan and manage risk will be enhanced through your studies.

I wish you the best of luck on the Risk Management Professional certification exam, should that be your goal. If you only use this book to improve your risk management skill set, I salute you! The desire to take your project management skills to a deeper level in the area of risk management is admirable. Study hard, prepare, and pass the test the first time!

This book is the second edition. It has been revised to reflect the latest PMI-RMP testing criteria. *Big* thanks to all who purchased our Version 1 edition! I think you'll find this second edition bigger and better.

Daniel C. Yeomans, MBA, PMI-RMP, PMI-PMP, PMI-ACP, CSM, CMQ/OE

---

[1] www.asq.org
[2] www.pmi.org

Acknowledgements

Nothing happens by coincidence. This is true in any life endeavor, including authoring and publishing a book such as this. I could acknowledge many contributors who made this book a reality, but that would take dozens of pages. Instead, I will acknowledge four contributors who helped me immensely along the way.

Patricia Carey, PMP

Patricia Carey, PMP, is a graduate of Northwest University in Kirkland, Washington. During the course of her studies, Patti was one of my students who took a total of nine semester hours in project management electives, graduated Summa Cum Laude, and attained her PMP certification. Patti played a critical role in proofreading and editing a 350-page Project Management Certification Prep Course that helped hundreds of professionals achieve PMP® or CAPM® certification.

Cynthia Holmberg, PMP, Certified Emergenetics Associate

Cynthia Holmberg, PMP, BA Business Management, Certified Emergenetics Associate, was a Learning and Development Consultant at Microsoft Corporation. She has over 30 years of experience in learning and development in the technology industry, focusing primarily on technical and project management training within the information technology (IT) environment. Cynthia worked with me to develop more than 30 project management-related courses over the past twelve years. Her feedback, insight, and great attention to detail allowed our development team to take all of the courses from good to great.

Peter Rogers, MBA

Peter Rogers, MBA, is a partner at P17 Group. Peter is a powerful coach who combines a strong academic background with years of high-impact training expertise helping individuals, teams, and organizations reach their potential. Peter is at the forefront of worldwide thinking on project management and program delivery. A Microsoft facilitator/trainer for more than 25 years, Peter is renowned for delivering Microsoft's project management courses and capabilities worldwide. Peter has also served as my development and facilitation partner for the past seventeen years. Many of the concepts in this book are a direct result of our brainstorming sessions and his expert insight.

Gilmere Vieira, PMP

Gilmere Vieira, PMP, was born in Brazil and moved to Seattle in 1990. Gilmere graduated Magna Cum Laude from the University of Washington with a BA in Business in 1997. She is currently working on her Leadership MBA at the University of Washington. She holds a PMP Certification, as well as a Dale Carnegie Effective Communications and Human Relations Certification. Gilmere worked closely with me over the years to improve project management competencies in the Microsoft Entertainment and Devices area. Through our mutual efforts, hundreds of Microsoft professionals achieved PMP or CAPM certification in her organization. She is a very valued partner!

Foreword

Most people live in the past or the future, not in the present. They stew over their past shortcomings and worry about what the future may bring. They do not pause to be in the present – to enjoy the present. Perhaps Project Managers are not like most people. Good Project Managers live more in the future, while attending to the present and mining the past for Lessons Learned. The future, or what may be, is, of course, the world of risk. Good Project Managers know that if they visualize what may be or what might happen, they will have a better and more manageable present. Why is this? Because the present, today, is influenced by how effectively we look forward to what might happen to our projects. These are, of course, the risks, both the good and the bad ones. Yes, there are good risks. What if we finish earlier than agreed and we actually delivered earlier than agreed? What could we do today, in the present, to increase the likelihood of this happening?

Currently, I am working on a project that has an inexperienced Sponsor. He is also hard to work with, and the project is destined for mediocrity or even failure. So what do I do? I have choices. We all have choices. I choose to have a good attitude – toward him, the project, and my work on the project. Rather than accept the status quo, I choose to influence his thinking and behavior so my work is likely to be much better on the project activities and the overall project. The risk is that the project may be mediocre or even fail, primarily due to an inexperienced Sponsor who is also hard to build a relationship with and work with. So, I re-envisioned this bad risk as a good risk. What can I do to influence the, thinking and behavior of the Project Sponsor to increase the likelihood of the project's success? At the end of the day, risk is a mindset. What is our attitude toward risk, and how can we turn negative risks to positive risks?

Unlike most people, the good Project Manager does not fear the future. Rather, they know that risk "is" – not to fear – rather, something to call out and deal with in a thoughtful and disciplined way. This leads me to Dan Yeomans and his wonderful book on risk. In this book, Dan deals with risk in both disciplined and insightful ways. He gives us everything we need to know about risk and to pass the Risk Management Professional certification exam *as well as* how to more successfully manage project risks for project success. You get not one but two great results! Moreover, the second result stays with you for your lifetime.

If you think about it, risk management is common sense. If we reduce or eliminate the bad risks, then our project will have smaller and fewer issues – those issues that cause projects to stray from their plans and to be less successful than originally agreed upon or expected. I call this the "Mark Twain School of Common Sense." Twain once said, "Success is more a function of common sense than it is of genius[3]." Again, risk management is common sense. Everyone does it all the time, some better than others. To become consistently good at it, read and apply what Dan presents so well in this book.

So, I urge you to join Dan and embrace risk. Become more disciplined with your common sense. You and your projects will be much more successful. How does 10% to 100% return on your investment sound? I know many people who would be content with a 7% return on their investments. So, have a go and enjoy the ride. Make it fun, apply the concepts and practices in this book to your projects and to your life. Attend to the future so that you may have a much better present.

Peter Rogers, Dan's friend and business colleague, and CEO, P17 Group LLC

---

[3] Brainyquote.com

About the Author

Daniel C. Yeomans became a Project Manager in 1977 while serving in the United States Air Force. Since that time, he has successfully coached, mentored, and trained thousands of Project Managers in a variety of settings.

Dan holds a Master's Degree in Business Administration (MBA) from St. Martin's University in Olympia, Washington. He is certified as a Project Management Professional (PMP), Agile Certified Practitioner (ACP), and Risk Management Professional (RMP) by the Project Management Institute (PMI). He is also recognized as a Certified ScrumMaster (CSM) and Certified Manager of Quality/Organizational Excellence (CMQ/OE). He also completed training to become an _Emergenetics_ Associate.

Dan is a member of the Project Management Institute (PMI) and the local PMI Puget Sound Chapter. He also uses his skills to support a number of non-profit organizations, including the Air Force Sergeants Association (AFSA).

Dan is currently working as an adjunct professor at Northwest University in Kirkland, Washington, supporting the institute's undergraduate- and graduate-level business programs. He is also a corporate trainer for Bellevue College and Green River College. His primary focus includes the project management and financial management curriculum areas. He also works as an independent consultant for P17 Group in the Seattle, Washington, area.

Dan developed more than 100 specific training offerings at both university and corporate levels. He developed a benchmark course and workbook for PMP certification that enabled hundreds at the university and corporate levels to successfully attain PMP or CAPM certification. He has a track record of success and seeks to share his successes with others using this book as a guide.

Introduction

Thank you for purchasing *Passing the Risk Management Professional (PMI-RMP)®
Certification Exam the First Time!* This is the second edition, and it covers the revised
domains and study references for the current test. The goal of this book is to prepare you to
achieve the Project Management Institute's Risk Management Professional Certification
(PMI-RMP) the first time. In addition, we are confident this book will give you some
greater insight into Risk Management best practices.

The PMI Risk Management Professional Credential was conceived in 2008. Once
achieved, this certification places you above the rest in terms of risk management
competency. The concepts covered in this book are appropriate for effective risk
management in project and non-project environments.

This book uses three key references as source documents:

1. *Project Management Body of Knowledge (PMBOK),*[4] 5th Edition. This book covers key
   project management concepts at a high level. Although the primary focus of *this*
   book is risk, it is highly advisable that PMI-RMP candidates have a basic
   understanding of project management principles in the *PMBOK*.

2. *Practice Standard for Project Risk Management*[5]. This is a great resource published by
   PMI. However, note that the information covered on the actual certification exam
   extends beyond the information provided in this publication.

3. *PMI Risk Management Professional (PMI-RMP) Exam Content Outline*[6]. This
   publication lists key objectives covered in the PMI-RMP certification exam. *This* risk
   management book maps to those objectives.

---

[4] PMBOK, 5th Edition
[5] PMI 2009 Edition
[6] PMI RMP Exam Content Outline 2012

Objectives

This book will explain and assist in understanding the six distinct steps of the PMI Risk Management Process, as defined in the 5th Edition of the *PMBOK*. We are confident you will gain a far greater understanding of a proven process to manage risk effectively as a result of reading this book. The PMI Risk Management Process defines key tools and techniques that can be applied to projects, thereby improving overall risk management skills.

This book is designed to help the reader recognize and accurately respond to questions regarding specific concepts addressed in each of the five domains of the RMP certification examination. In this edition, you have access to:

- A series of activities designed to prepare you for the PMI-RMP certification exam. We encourage you to complete each Activity. Activity solutions are located in Appendix A.

- A 150-question "final test" you can use to check your readiness to challenge the PMI-RMP certification examination. This test covers key risk management objectives stated in PMI literature. It also covers questions in other areas of project management you may encounter on the test. For example, Earned Value Technique is a certification objective covered in this book.

- A list of acronyms used in this book in Appendix C. Acronyms are often used on the certification exam in place of the written-out definition. For example, WBS is more commonly used instead of spelling out Work Breakdown Structure. Acronyms must be understood.

- A comprehensive glossary of terms used in this book for your reference in Appendix D.

- A number of *italicized* entries. These entries are important concepts that will likely appear on the certification exam.

- Key concepts are repeated more than once throughout this book. This is by design. Repetition enhances understanding and learning.

The PMI Risk Management Professional Certification Exam

The PMI Risk Management Professional Body of Knowledge includes five key areas, or domains. The PMI-RMP certification exam covers all five domains. An in-depth understanding of risk management activities that support each area is critical to pass the certification exam.

The Five Domains of Project Risk Management

Here is a list of the five key domains of concentration:

1. **Risk Strategy and Planning**: This area includes 19% to 20% of all certification exam questions. Risk Strategy and Planning questions can support all six Project Risk Management activities, as listed in the *PMBOK* 5th Edition. We will focus on the Plan Risk Management Process as the primary source to understand this domain. PMI specifically defines five tasks that must be understood in the Risk Strategy and Planning domain as follows:

Tasks	Domain 1: Description of Risk Strategy and Planning Tasks
1.	Develop risk assessment processes and tools that quantify stakeholder risk tolerances in order to assess and determine risk thresholds for the project and set criteria for risk levels.
2.	Update risk policies and procedures using information such as lessons learned from projects and outputs of risk audits in order to improve risk management effectiveness.
3.	Develop and recommend project risk strategy based on project objectives in order to establish the outline for the risk management plan.
4.	Produce risk management plan for the project on the basis of inputs such as project information, external factors, stakeholder inputs, and industry policies and procedures in order to define, fund, and staff effective risk management processes that align with other project plans.
5.	Establish evaluation criteria for risk management processes based on project baselines and objectives in order to measure effectiveness of the project risk process.

2. **Stakeholder Engagement**: The Stakeholder Engagement domain includes 19% to 20% of all certification exam questions and concentrates on multiple areas covered in the *PMBOK*. You need to understand nine distinct tasks, as PMI specifically defines nine tasks that must be understood in the Stakeholder Engagement domain. Pay close attention to Chapter 9, Project Stakeholder Management. We share many key knowledge areas that are addressed in this domain.

Tasks	Domain 2: Description of Stakeholder Engagement Tasks
1.	Promote a common understanding of the value of risk management by using interpersonal skills in order to foster an appropriate level of shared accountability, responsibility, and risk ownership.
2.	Train, coach, and educate stakeholders in risk principles and processes in order to create shared understanding of principles and processes, and foster engagement in risk management.
3.	Coach project team members in implementing risk processes in order to ensure the consistent application of risk processes.
4.	Assess stakeholder risk tolerance using processes and tools such as interviewing stakeholders and reviewing historical stakeholder behaviors in order to identify risk thresholds.
5.	Identify stakeholder risk attitudes and cognitive biases using stakeholder analysis techniques in order to manage stakeholder expectations and responses throughout the life of the project.
6.	Engage stakeholders on risk prioritization process based on stakeholder risk tolerance and other relevant criteria, in order to optimize consensus regarding priorities.
7.	Provide risk-related recommendations to stakeholders regarding risk strategy and planning, risk process facilitation, risk reporting, and specialized risk tasks by using effective communications techniques in order to support effective risk-based decision making.
8.	Promote risk ownership by proactively communicating roles and responsibilities and engaging project team members in the development of risk responses in order to improve risk response execution.
9.	Liaise with stakeholders of other projects by using effective communication techniques and sharing information on project risk performance in order to inform them of implications for their projects.

3. **Risk Process Facilitation**: The Risk Process Facilitation domain includes 25% to 28% of all certification exam questions. This area covers multiple processes within the Project Risk Management knowledge area of the *PMBOK*. PMI specifically defines seven tasks that must be understood in the Risk Process Facilitation domain.

Tasks	Domain 3: Description of Risk Process Facilitation Domain Tasks
1.	Apply risk assessment processes and tools in order to quantify stakeholder risk tolerances and determine risk levels.
2.	Facilitate risk identification using a number of techniques in order to enable the project team and stakeholders to understand and determine the risk exposure of the project.
3.	Facilitate the project team's evaluation of the identified risks' attributes using qualitative and quantitative tools and techniques in order to prioritize the risks for response planning.
4.	Facilitate the development of the aligned risk response strategy and related risk actions by risk owners from the information gathered during risk analysis in order to ensure timely and defined action when required.
5.	Facilitate the formulation of project contingency reserve based on the risk exposure of the project in order to have the capability and resources to respond to realized risks.
6.	Provide risk data to cost and schedule analysts/estimators to ensure that project risk is properly reflected in cost and schedule estimates for the project.
7.	Use scenarios to validate potential risk responses and evaluate key dependencies and requirements in order to enhance the likelihood of project success.

4. **Risk Monitoring and Reporting**: This domain includes 19% to 20% of all certification exam questions. This area covers concepts in the Control Risks process, along with many other knowledge areas in the *PMBOK*. PMI specifically defines seven tasks that must be understood in the Risk Monitoring and Reporting domain.

Tasks	Domain 4: Description of Risk Monitoring and Reporting Domain Tasks
1.	Document and periodically update project risk information using standard tools (including but not limited to risk register, risk database) and techniques in order to maintain a single, current repository of all project risk information.
2.	Coordinate with project manager using communication techniques in order to integrate risk management throughout the project.
3.	Create periodic standard and custom reports using risk-related metrics as specified in the risk management plan in order to communicate risk management activities and status.
4.	Monitor risk response metrics by analyzing risk response performance information and present to key stakeholders in order to ensure resolution of risk and develop additional risk response strategies to address residual and secondary risks.
5.	Analyze risk process performance against established metrics in order to drive risk process improvements.
6.	Update the project risk management plan using relevant internal and external inputs in order to keep the plan current.
7.	Capture risk lessons learned through comprehensive review of the project risk management plan, risk register, risk audits, risk process performance reports, and other associated reports in order to incorporate into future risk planning.

5. **Perform Specialized Risk Analysis**: This domain includes 14% to 16% of all certification exam questions. This area covers multiple quantitative and statistical analysis tools and techniques used to analyze risks. PMI specifically defines three tasks that must be understood in the Perform Specialized Risk Analysis domain.

Tasks	Domain 5: Description of Perform Specialized Risk Analysis Domain Tasks
1.	Evaluate the attributes of identified risks using advanced quantitative tools and specialized qualitative techniques in order to estimate overall risk exposure of the project.
2.	Analyze risk data produced during the project using statistical analyses and expert judgement in order to determine strengths and weaknesses of risk strategy and processes and recommend process improvement when indicated.
3.	Perform specialized risk analysis using advanced tools and techniques in order to support stakeholder decision making for the project.

To Qualify for Testing

You must complete an application through the Project Management Institute to qualify for the PMI-RMP certification examination[7]. You may complete a paper or online application. The application must show you have adequate education and experience in the risk management area of project management to qualify to take the test.

The PMI-RMP certification is a stand-alone credential. It is administered in English only. You may take the test up to three times in a one-year period to attain a passing score. The ability to test is not impacted by any other PMI certifications you may possess.

---

[7] www.pmi.org

The table below provides an overview of the required education and experience needed to qualify for PMI-RMP testing:

Education	Project Risk Experience	Project Risk Management Education
High school diploma, Associates Degree, or global equivalent	At least 4,500 hours spent in the specialized area of professional project risk management within the last 5 consecutive years	40 contact hours of formal education in the specialized area of Project Risk Management
OR		
Bachelor's Degree or global equivalent	At least 3,000 hours spent in the specialized area of professional project risk management within the last 5 consecutive years	30 contact hours of formal education in the specialized area of Project Risk Management

About the Test

You will be authorized to take the PMI-RMP certification exam after your application is approved by PMI. Here are specifics that describe the certification exam process:

- The test is computerized. All questions are multiple choices, with four potential answers. Each question has only one correct answer. Most test questions are short and very straight forward. Some include extraneous verbiage designed to distract. Always try to understand what the question is asking before responding.

- You will have time to write down notes before you start the test. You will be offered an opportunity to take a 15-minute tutorial on how to use the computerized testing system. You will also be given pencils and note paper or equivalent you can use during the test. This tutorial should not take more than two to three minutes to complete. It is my recommendation that you take advantage of time remaining to write down key pieces of information before you begin the actual test. You may want to consider the following tips, at a minimum:

  o List the six steps of Project Risk Management in the order they occur.

- o List key inputs, tools and techniques, and outputs for all Project Risk Management activities.

- o List key formulas such as Earned Value Technique, Expected Monetary Value, etc.

- o List key definitions you may wish to reference during the test.

- The test consists of 170 questions. Of these, 150 questions are graded. The other 20 questions are "pre-release" and are not graded. You will not be able to identify the pre-release questions. Therefore, answer all questions to the best of your ability.

- You have 3.5 hours to complete the test. You will have the option to mark questions you want to review before you finalize the test.

  - o It is a best practice to go through the test one time and answer questions you are sure of first. Then come back to answer the more difficult questions. You can mark questions you wish to review later.

  - o Take a periodic break during the test. Many certification professionals recommend you take a short break for a few minutes every 50 questions to catch your breath and refresh yourself.

- Testing is conducted at designated testing centers. You are able to schedule your own testing time at the center of your choice after your application is approved.

- A calculator is provided for math questions. You will be provided either a hand held calculator or one that is included on the computer.

- Ensure you have two picture IDs when you arrive at the testing center. A locker will be provided for you to store any personal items.

- PMI has not published a passing score for the PMI-RMP credential. Therefore, strive for a 75% score on all practice tests provided in this book.

- You will be notified of your pass/fail status at the completion of the exam. You will be given a scorecard that shows your proficiency levels in each of the five domains of the PMI-RMP Body of Knowledge.

- You will be required to attain 30 Professional Development Units (PDUs) over a three-year period to maintain the certification after you pass the test.

Note: Should you have any questions or need assistance, please contact me at Dan@P17Group.com. I will do my best to assist you on your PMI-RMP journey.

As a bonus, if you purchase this book, you are authorized to go to our website at www.p17group.com. We have a variety of proven project management tools and techniques available for your review and use. For example, in this book we discuss Risk Management Plans, Risk Registers, etc., from a conceptual standpoint. Go to our website for some real-world examples you can download and use.

Template Access Code

When you go to our website, www.p17group.com, our templates and examples are waiting for you. Please use the code below for access.

Access Code:
060110

Chapter 1: The Risk Management Process

The Risk Management Process in the *PMBOK* is a six-step taxonomy designed to help manage end-to-end project risk. An acronym we developed to remember the process steps in order is PIER-C. This acronym stands for Plan, Identify, Evaluate, Respond, and Control.

Project Risk Management is a very challenging process. However, practice makes perfect. The Risk Management Process is designed to follow a proven formula for success. That formula is Plan-Do-Check-Act, or PDCA. Success in project management is best achieved when you *Plan* before you *Do*. As you *Do* the project, you *Check* to ensure the plan is being followed. If there are issues, you must *Act* accordingly. Believe it or not, risk management becomes easier the more it is performed.

Risk Definition

Project Risk is defined in the *PMBOK* as, "An uncertain event or condition that, if it occurs, has a positive or negative effect on at least one of the project's objectives." *Project objectives* are defined as *scope, time, cost,* and *quality*.

Recurrent projects generally have the best understood risks. Complex projects with many unknowns are far more challenging, from a risk standpoint.

PMI developed a six-step process to effectively manage project risk. This process is highlighted in Figure 1.1. It works!

Figure 1.1 PMI Risk Management Process

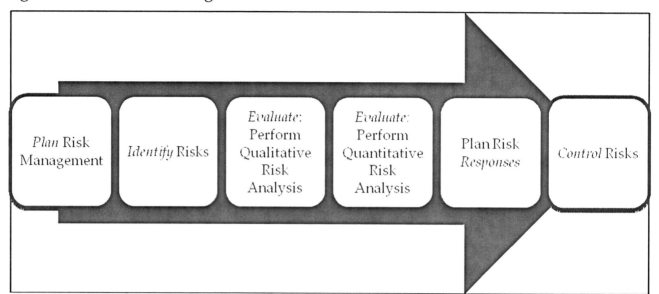

The PMI Risk Management Process: An Overview of PIER-C

I developed the "PIER-C" process which correlates with the PMI six-step process in Figure 1.1. The "PIER" process activities or steps occur during the Project Planning Process group. The Control Risks process occurs during the Project Monitoring and Controlling Process group. This is the "C", which combine to create PIER-C. Here is a quick overview of each step in the order they occur. As a testing note, memorize and understand this order.

1. **Plan Risk Management:** This initial process defines how risk management will be accomplished (methodology). The ultimate goal is to develop a Risk Management Plan that describes how the entire end-to-end Risk Management Process will work.

2. **Identify Risks:** This process requires you to develop a list of risks by project, activity, work package, etc. During this step, you define the risk, assign initial ownership, define risk causes, develop initial responses, and categorize each risk. The key output of the Identify Risks process is a document called the Risk Register.

3. **Perform Qualitative Risk Analysis:** This is the first evaluation process, and it is *subjective*. During this step, you use the Risk Register to classify risks by *probability* (likelihood the risk will occur) and *impact* (effect of the risk consequence on the project). At the end of this step, prioritize all risks and establish a short list of risks that must be aggressively managed. This is often referred to as the Urgent List. You also place low probability and low impact risks in a separate section of the Risk Register. This is called a Watch List. The Risk Register is updated at the conclusion of this step.

4. **Perform Quantitative Risk Analysis:** This process is *optional*. The Project Manager decides! You may or may not perform the Quantitative Risk Analysis process. This decision is determined by factors such as time, project priority, level of effort as compared to benefits, etc. This evaluation method numerically analyzes the impact of multiple risks to the project. This is an *objective* method that helps determine probability that stated budgetary and schedule outcomes can be met. The Risk Register is updated at the conclusion of this step.

5. **Plan Risk Responses:** The next process in the Risk Management Process is Plan Risk Responses. During this step, develop responses to risks on the urgent, or "short," list of risks. The level of response detail is dictated by the priority of the risk. Strive for responses that address both positive risks (opportunities) and negative risks (threats). The Risk Register is updated at the conclusion of this step. In addition, contractual agreements may be developed to support responses that require third-party involvement.

6. **Control Risks:** This is the final process in the Risk Management Process. During this step, monitor and reassess risks on the Risk Register. Implement risk responses, as necessary. Identify new or Emergent Risks that were not identified during the Identify Risks process. In addition, evaluate the effectiveness of the risk program for the overall project. Look for Triggers, early warning signs a risk has or will occur. The Risk Register is updated during this step as well.

Performing Risk Activities

Each process in the Project Risk Management knowledge area follows a three-step approach as shown in Figure 1.2. The approach consists of gathering *Inputs*, using *Tools and Techniques* to transform the inputs, and completing the activity by generating *Outputs*.

Figure 1.2 Risk Process Approach

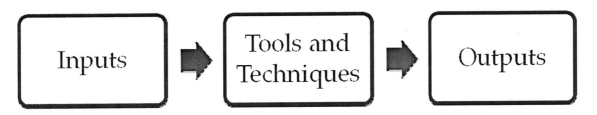

- **Inputs**: Always begin each process by gathering required inputs and providing them to the Risk Team members performing the activity. Think of inputs as what you would bring to a planning meeting.

- **Tools and Techniques**: Ensure all Risk Team members are aware of the types of tools and techniques that will be used. These tools and techniques are used to transform inputs into outputs. Some tools and techniques work better than others, depending on the type of project and team. Some tools and techniques may require specific training.

- **Outputs**: Use the appropriate tools and techniques to generate required outputs. This is the deliverable or product take-away from the meeting.

Other Basic Concepts to Remember

- **Project Risk Management Process**: The Project Risk Management Process aims to help control projects by reducing uncertainties or unknowns. Two key areas that cause risks are assumptions or estimates. Identifying as many risks as possible is a highly recommended best practice. *There are two types of risks—known risks and unknown risks.* You can manage risks you know about. Unknown risks are not easily identified and often occur at the most inopportune times. Find all the risks, or they will find you!

  o The PMI-RMP methodology focuses on single projects. The published methodology does not focus on *portfolios* or *programs*. A portfolio is a group of programs or projects grouped together to facilitate management of the work. A program is a group of related projects.

  o Risk management identifies and analyzes *individual risks* and *overall project risk*. Overall project risk is quantified using a Project Risk Score. This score reflects the uncertainty of the project as a whole by adding the total of all individual Risk Scores.

  o Risk management should be conducted in accordance with existing corporate policies and procedures.

  o *Assumptions* are defined as information believed to be true. A key risk management success factor is to understand assumptions and validate them. Disconnects between project plans and assumptions are indicators of project risk.

o The objectives of risk management are to increase the probability and impact of positive events and decrease the probability and impact of negative events. The aim is to identify and prioritize risks before they occur and provide action-oriented information concerning risk to all key stakeholders.

o Risk management includes all activities concerned with conducting the six end-to-end processes that comprise the PMI Project Risk Management methodology.

o Project Risk Management is *not* an optional activity. PMI states that risk management activities must be applied to every project.

- **Risk Attitudes/Tolerance/Thresholds:** The overall *risk attitudes* of stakeholders determine the significance and priority of both individual risks and overall project risk. These attitudes can be impacted by the priority of the project, level of commitment, sensitivity to certain types of risk, overall organizational culture, etc.

  o It is critical to understand stakeholder attitudes toward risk *before* undertaking risk identification activities.

  o Risk attitude can affect measurements of risk probability and impact. In addition, risk attitudes can impact the ability to procure Contingency Reserves to address risk events. For example, stakeholders may have a high tolerance for budget overruns. If this is the case, budget-related risks should not be prioritized as high as other risks.

  o A *tolerance* is normally broad. For example, stakeholders have a low tolerance for schedule delays. A *threshold* is normally a numeric indicator of tolerance. For example, the schedule cannot slip by more than three days.

- **Positive and Negative Risks**: Risks can be either positive or negative. Negative risks are referred to as *threats*. Positive risks are referred to as *opportunities*.

- **Timing:** Risk management is not a one-time event. It is *iterative*. It must be repeated throughout the life of a project. You will identify new risks as the project progresses. Emergent Risks are defined as risks not identified initially. These are risks discovered after the project begins. In addition, risks initially identified may become candidates for closure and deletion from the Risk Register.

- o The level of *Risk Exposure*, or risk impacting a project, is always highest at the beginning of the project. When new or Emergent Risks are identified, a best practice is to look for additional related risks.

- o The risk of not successfully completing a project peaks during the Project Initiation Process Group. Risk Exposure is reduced through solid risk management as the project progresses. The potential for project success increases when risks are identified early in the project management process.

- o The level of risk management depth and level of effort should be scaled and tailored to the project. Extensive risk management activities may be appropriate for some projects but not others.

- **Risk Categories:** Placing risks in categories identifies common causes and facilitates better risk responses. PMI lists two types of risks:

  - o *Business Risks*: These risks can either be opportunities or threats. They can result in either profit or loss.

  - o *Insurable Risks*: These are also called *Pure Risks*. Insurable risks are always negative or threats. In addition, they are outside the Project Manager's control. Examples are natural disasters, fire, theft, etc.

- **Issues and Benefits**: Risks are potential events that have not occurred. A negative risk that occurs is called an *issue or problem*. A positive event that occurs is called a *benefit*. All issues and benefits should be documented in a formal Issues Log.

- **PMO Role**: A Project Management Office, or PMO, can play a role in risk management. The PMO is an organization that could share policies, procedures, templates, etc. A PMO traditionally supports project management in the organization. This includes risk management. There may be a specific *Risk Management Department* assigned to your organization to specifically address risk management.

Risk Management: Keys to Success

Listed below are key success factors that impact the success of a risk management program.

- *Value of Risk Management*: It is imperative to ensure all stakeholders understand the value of an effective Project Risk Management program and the return on investment from a stakeholder's level of effort. If this objective is not met, resistance from stakeholders can be expected. The Project Manager is responsible to ensure stakeholder buy-in.

- *Stakeholder and Organizational Commitment*: All stakeholders must be committed to perform their roles and responsibilities supporting effective risk management. The organization must be committed to risk management as a whole.

- *Communication*: Open and honest communication is key to success. Include all key stakeholders in the Project Communications Plan to ensure maximum risk management effectiveness.

- *Integration:* Risk management must be integrated with all project management activities to be successful. Risk management cannot be an isolated event.

- **Reserves:** It is important to plan for *reserves* to address risks. Reserves are simply extra time or costs added to the project baseline to account for risks. Effective risk management provides a basis for identifying and requesting reserves. There are two types of reserves:

  o *Contingency Reserves*: These reserves account for *known risks*.

  o *Management Reserves*: These are reserves for *unknown risks*.

  o Reserves are normally determined by guessing (believe it or not), using an x% rule (normally 10%), using Expected Monetary Value, or through computerized What If Scenario Analysis, such as *Monte Carlo*.

- **The Seven Constraint Model**: According to PMI, seven constraints drive risk tolerance levels. This model is highlighted in Figure 1.3. Revisiting this model will prove beneficial. This model supplements traditional constraints of scope, time, and cost with resources, risk, quality, and customer satisfaction. It is used to describe stakeholder risk tolerance areas.

Figure 1.3 Seven Constraint Model

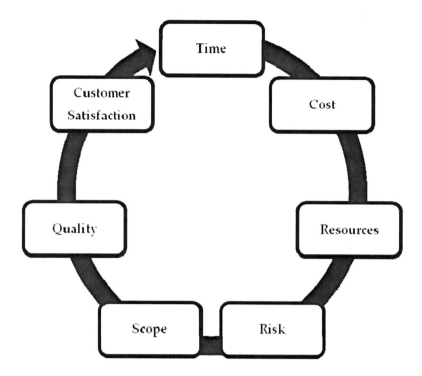

Project Manager's Role in Risk Management

The Project Manager ensures Project Risk Management is accomplished at an appropriate level to ensure project success. They are accountable to ensure all required processes are followed.

Here are some specific Project Manager responsibilities:

- Manage risk on a daily basis from the Initiating Process Group through Closing Process Group.

- Ensure a Risk Management Plan is developed and approved. Promote the need to have and follow a Risk Management Process.

- Include risk as part of periodic project status meetings. Communicate risk status to all key stakeholders.

- Ensure risk is communicated effectively. Ensure risk is included as part of the overall Project Communications Management Plan. Strive for open and honest communications.

- Encourage senior management to support the Risk Management Process. Share the benefits of adopting a solid Risk Management Process.

- Understand stakeholder attitudes, tolerances, and thresholds. These factors impact risk prioritization, response strategies, and reserve requirements.

- Approve risk responses. Escalate responses as required. Ensure risk responses are approved and incorporated into the Project Management Plan.

Activity 1: Risk Management Process Overview

Directions: Read the twelve true or false questions below. Answers are in Appendix A.

	Question	True or False
1.	Project risk is normally highest during the project Executing Process Group.	
2.	The first step in the Risk Management Process is Identify Risks.	
3.	The Plan Risk Responses process occurs in the Project Planning Process Group.	
4.	Three of the most common constraints that determine stakeholder tolerance levels include scope, resources, and stakeholder expectations.	
5.	The Project Manager must attempt to attain an organizational commitment to the value of risk management.	
6.	Management Reserves are defined as reserves to address unknown risks.	
7.	A risk that is identified early in the Risk Management Process is called an Emergent Risk.	
8.	The Perform Quantitative Risk Analysis process is mandatory. It is a subjective analysis method.	
9.	Stakeholder risk attitudes and tolerances can impact overall risk prioritization and response efforts.	
10.	The Risk Register is developed as part of the Plan Risk Management process of Project Risk Management.	
11.	Insurable, or Pure Risks, can be both negative and positive.	
12.	When a positive risk occurs, it is referred to as a benefit.	

Chapter 2: Plan Risk Management Process

Process 1: Plan Risk Management

Plan Risk Management is the first process in the project Risk Management. The ultimate goal is to define processes and a strategy to guide the end-to-end Project Risk Management Process in a Risk Management Plan. Note that the majority of tasks in Domain 1 are covered in this Chapter. At a high level, the Plan Risk Management process provides:

- A tailored Risk Management Process and strategy applicable to the project and adapted to meet stakeholder requirements, expectations, and attitudes.

- Rules that will govern and guide the execution of all Project Risk Management Processes. Direction on how Project Risk Management will be integrated with all other project management processes.

- Key thresholds that will guide subsequent risk management activities.

Plan Risk Management Process

The Plan Risk Management process consists of inputs, tools and techniques, and outputs. Figure 2.1 provides an overview of this process.

Figure 2.1 Plan Risk Management Process

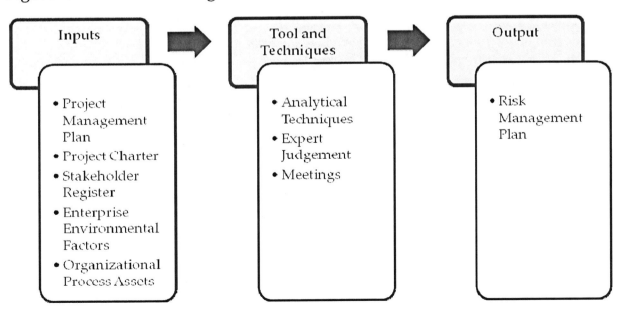

Plan Risk Management: Inputs

A number of inputs are required to accomplish the Plan Risk Management process. Each of these inputs will improve the overall quality of the Risk Management Plan.

- **Project Management Plan**: The Risk Management Plan will be a component of the overall Project Management Plan that must be approved by a Sponsor and accepted by stakeholders before it is finalized as the Project Baseline. Policies and processes to integrate risk planning into all phases of the Project Management Plan development must be defined. A point to remember: **Sponsor Approval + Stakeholder Acceptance = Project Baseline.**

- **Project Charter**: Project Risk Management begins with the development of the Project Charter. High level risks defined in the Project Charter must be considered. In addition, stakeholder expectations defined in the Project Charter will impact risk planning in terms of goals, measurements of success, tolerances, etc.

- **Stakeholder Register**: It is the Project Manager's responsibility to control Project Risk Management and include all stakeholders in the end-to-end planning process. Stakeholder inputs to ensure the Risk Management Plan meets the needs of the project is essential. The Stakeholder Register provides a list of those stakeholders impacted or interested in the project. In addition, a Stakeholder Register should define current levels of stakeholder commitment to determine measures that must be taken if any. See Chapter 9 for more information on this key criterion.

- **Enterprise Environmental Factors:** *By definition, Enterprise Environmental Factors are conditions not under the immediate control of the team that influence, constrain, or potentially guide the project's direction.* Factors such as systems, values, and culture are Enterprise Environmental Factors that must be recognized and managed. Risk attitudes and tolerances and the degree of risk an organization is willing to tolerate are keys to effective risk planning.

- **Organizational Process Assets:** *This list includes plans, processes, policies, procedures, and knowledge bases that are specific to an organization.* Organizational Process Assets can lead to potential risks and must be identified during the risk planning process. Key Organizational Process Assets that need to be considered include Lessons Learned, historical information, required templates, etc.

Plan Risk Management: Tools and Techniques

Three tools and techniques use the inputs to the Plan Risk Management process and pave the way for the completion of a comprehensive Risk Management Plan. Let's review each one.

- **Meetings:** Conducting planning meetings is the responsibility of the Project Manager. A best practice to ensure a quality result is to invite key stakeholders to participate in the meetings. A Risk Team may be assigned to your project. These are individuals who are specifically assigned risk management activities. They should be part of all planning meetings as well.

  o Meeting participants should include the Project Manager, selected team members, other key stakeholders, selected Subject Matter Experts (SMEs), and stakeholders with risk management responsibilities on the Risk Team.

  o Discussions at the initial planning meeting may include risk responsibilities, definitions of methodology, clarification of definitions and terms, and the impact of risks on project objectives. In addition, standard templates that will be used should be explained and introduced. Future meetings will likely be required to help finalize the Risk Management Plan.

- **Expert Judgement:** There is a saying I've coined that states the essence of Expert Judgement. "Know what you know, know what you don't know, and surround yourself with people who know what you don't know." We shared earlier that there are two types of risks, known and unknown. The most dangerous type is the unknown risk. You may not find them, but in all likelihood, they will find you! Surround yourself with experts who can help you turn the unknown into the known. If you know about a risk, you can develop a response to address it.

- **Analytical Techniques:** Effective analysis of people, tools, and business factors need to be considered as you develop your Risk Management Plan.

  o *People:* People considerations may include risk attitudes, tolerances, and thresholds. It is highly recommended that risk management roles and responsibilities be defined. Another people consideration is communications. A methodology for communicating risk should be considered, discussed, defined, and used throughout the project. The result of these conversations should be reflected in the project Communications Management Plan.

o *Tools:* There are many tools that can be used to support the overall Plan Risk Management process. This includes rules of use, definitions, terms, etc. Matching the right tool and technique to the right process is also highly recommended.

o *Business:* Any key constraints or boundaries should be addressed and documented. Priority of scope, time, and cost should be documented and agreed upon. These priorities will impact future risk prioritization activities. In addition, the amount of effort planned for expenditure on risk management based on the project's attributes must be considered as well.

Plan Risk Management Output: Risk Management Plan

The Risk Management Plan guides the end-to end Risk Management Process for the project. It defines pertinent terminology and *ensures shared understanding and buy-in of terms and methodology.* In addition, it defines roles, responsibilities, and advises stakeholders of specifics regarding expected involvement.

The Risk Management Plan addresses two types of criteria:

- *Project-Related Criteria*: What are the required results for cost, time, scope, and quality? How can risk impact these results?

- *Process-Related Criteria*: What are the key processes that must be followed to ensure success? What are the risks that may impact these processes?

There are challenges and barriers to effective risk management. Here are a few tips to manage these challenges:

- Share the benefits of solid risk management to stakeholders. Ensure stakeholders are aware of the overall benefits of participating in risk management activities.

- Ensure a clear definition of the project's objectives is understood and agreed upon by all stakeholders.

- Be aware of Enterprise Environmental Factors that can impact risk negatively or positively. Identify pertinent Organizational Process Assets ahead of time.

The Risk Management Plan becomes part of the Project Baseline and *must be approved by the Project Sponsor.* The table that follows provides a breakout of recommended entries.

Risk Management Plan Consideration	Comments
Methodology	What approach will be used to manage risk? What tools or data sources might be leveraged? Consider a Risk Breakdown Structure (RBS).
Roles and Responsibilities	Define lead support and team membership for risk planning. Define the Risk Team.
Budgeting	How will the cost of risk be incorporated in the Cost Performance Baseline? How will Contingency Planning occur?
Timing	How often will risk management be performed? Weekly is the norm.
Risk Categories	Which risk categories impact the project? A common method is assigning risk by time, scope, quality, and/or cost.
Definitions of Probability and Impact	Probability equals the chances a risk event will occur. Impact equals the consequences of the risk event to the project. Be able to define both and determine how risks will be prioritized based on these indicators.
Probability and Impact Matrix	Tool used to determine how much management effort you will exert on a given risk. It generally differentiates risks by Risk Score as High, Moderate, or Low. This tool is used during the Perform Qualitative Risk Analysis process.
Stakeholder Attitudes, Tolerances and Thresholds	What levels of risk are acceptable? • Attitudes impact tolerances, thresholds, and expected levels of commitment and support. What are the factors to be considered? • Tolerance is a measure of risk levels that management is willing to accept. Use the Seven Constraint model. • Thresholds are specific ranges, i.e., variations between + or − 5%.

Reporting Formats	Reports, templates, documents used to record and communicate risk?
Tracking	How will risk activities be recorded and shared? How will the risk process be audited? How will Lessons Learned be captured and shared?

Plan Risk Management: Other Key Concepts

- *Risk Breakdown Structure (RBS):* Many organizations use an RBS that lists risk *categories and sub-categories in hierarchical order* to help identify risks. An RBS places risks in categories and defines specific risks applicable to the type of project being managed in that category. An example of an RBS that shows financial risks follows:

Financial			
Factor	**Low Risk**	**Medium Risk**	**High Risk**
Return	Returns on this and similar projects will be calculated, and exceed the financial criteria. Cash inflow will be large and early in the project life.	Returns on this project will be assessed to be within normal business practices. Cash flow will be continuous throughout the project life.	Returns on this project will be subject to major assumptions and wide variances in possible outcomes. Cash flow is uncertain. Returns cannot be easily measured.
Costs	All costs are known. Costs are set and not expected to exceed budget.	Cost estimates for some components are not known or not quantified.	Cost analysis has not been done. Estimates are difficult to attain.
Budget Size	Sufficient budget is allocated.	Questionable budget allocated.	Doubtful budget is sufficient.
Budget Constraints	Funds allocated without constraints.	Some questions about availability of funds.	Source of funds in doubt or subject to change without notice.
Cost Controls	Well established and in place.	System in place, weak in some areas.	System lacking or nonexistent.

- *Assumptions:* The Risk Management Plan should include a process to validate assumptions. Remember that an assumption is something believed to be true, but not yet confirmed.

- *Constraints:* Constraints are defined as anything that might limit the team's options. Constraints are boundaries that must be acknowledged and addressed. The seven-sided constraint model shared earlier provides categories of constraints that should be considered.

- There is key terminology to consider in this step as well:

  o *Risk Tolerance Areas:* These are areas where key stakeholders are willing to accept risk. These areas should be identified.

  o *Risk Averse:* This indicates a stakeholder's unwillingness to accept risk.

  o *Risk Thresholds:* This is a measure of the risk a stakeholder is willing to accept. Risk thresholds can be a percentage or a figure such as +/- 1 week, etc. Risk thresholds help determine the responses to risk events.

  o *Risk Utility:* The Risk Utility function describes a person or organization's willingness to accept risk.

Plan Risk Management: Keys to Success

- *Look for and Address Barriers:* Identify barriers or factors that may impact the Risk Management Process.

- *Define Project Objectives:* Define objectives to include time, cost, scope, and quality that may be impacted by risk as accurately and clearly as possible. See Figure 2.2. Avoid ambiguity.

Figure 2.2 Key Project Objectives

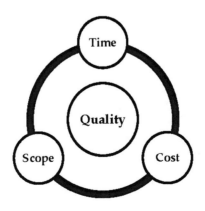

- *Stakeholder Involvement*: Do not develop a Risk Management Plan without soliciting input and perspectives from multiple sources. Gain commitment and buy in.

- *Measure Stakeholder tolerance levels and thresholds*: Develop tools or methods to determine the tolerance and threshold levels of stakeholders.

  - Lessons Learned: Review Lessons Learned to determine where stakeholder focus was highest. Was there more concern for scope, time, or cost?

  - Project Charter: Many experienced Project Managers define the priorities for meeting scope, time, and cost in the Project Charter. This method allows you to confirm what is most important, and focus your risk planning and management efforts accordingly. Your overall risk strategy should be based on the priority of meeting project objectives.

  - Surveys and Questionnaires: Questions stakeholders—you may get an answer. Determine their willingness to accept risk in multiple areas, and plan accordingly.

- *Policy and Procedure:* Many organizations have established policy and procedures that may impact how project risk management is performed. The Project Manager needs to review Lessons Learned, results of past Risk Audits, and recommend updates to policy when applicable. This policy and procedure should be reflected in the project Risk Management Plan. **Note:** A Risk Audit is a review of a risk response when a risk occurs. We cover this concept later under the Control Risks process.

- *Compliance*: Ensure key organizational policies and procedures are adhered to. Accommodate key governance criteria and methods.

- *Categorization*: Categorizing risks allows the ability to group risks based on common causes. Categorization improves the quality of risk responses.

- *Organizational Process Assets*: Ensure key templates, historical records, Lessons Learned, etc. are understood and leveraged. Make certain all the inputs you need are available to develop a viable Risk Management Plan.

- *Share the Risk Management Plan*: Share the plan with all stakeholders. Ensure the plan becomes part of the overall Project Management Plan. Ensure the Risk Management Plan reflects the following:

    o Project Information: Plan must reflect realistic time, cost, and scope objectives

    o External Factors: Any external constraints such as regulations, politics, environmental conditions, etc. that may impact project results

    o Industry Policies and Procedures: Any external or internal industry policy or procedures that may impact how the project is managed, and potential project results.

    o Measurement: The plan should show how you will quantitatively measure risk for the project to determine effectiveness of the overall risk management function. We will discuss how using overall Risk Scores can assist you later in the book.

    o Alignment: Ensure the plan aligns with the realities of other projects. Individual projects are rarely managed in a vacuum.

Activity 2: Plan Risk Management Process

Directions: A number of key definitions and concepts should be understood. Match the scenario or definition to the potential responses provided.

Plan Risk Management Definition and Concept Activity	Response
1. A tool and technique used in the Plan Risk Management process that encourages you to seek the help of multiple stakeholders when planning risk.	
2. A term that describes a measure of the amount or range of risk a stakeholder is willing to tolerate.	
3. A practice that allows for identification of risks with common causes that normally leads to more effective responses.	
4. Any factor that can limit the team's options. Boundaries that must be addressed and planned.	
5. A key deliverable that defines the overall strategy to be used to support the project's end-to-end Risk Management Process.	
6. Key input to the Plan Risk Management process. Includes Lessons Learned, stakeholder tolerance information, templates, policies, and/or procedures.	
7. A tool that provides a hierarchical breakout of potential risks by category. Shows potential risks and risk thresholds for risks within each category.	
8. Something the team believes to be true but has not yet validated.	
9. Areas where key stakeholders are willing to accept risk.	
10. A key input to the Plan Risk management process that defines key stakeholders, their roles, and the current commitment level they possess.	
11. Conditions not under the immediate control of the team. A common process input. Specifically culture, systems, and values.	
12. Term that describes a person or organization's willingness to accept risk.	

Activity 2: Choose from the following:

A. Organizational Process Assets

B. Categorization

C. Risk Threshold

D. Assumption

E. Risk Management Plan

F. Risk Breakdown Structure (RBS)

G. Expert Judgement

H. Constraints

I. Risk Tolerance Areas

J. Stakeholder Register

K. Enterprise Environmental Factors

L. Risk Utility

Chapter 3: Identify Risks Process

Process 2: Identify Risks

Identify Risks is the second step in Project Risk Management. The ultimate output of Identify Risks is the initial Risk Register. This output records risks and their characteristics.

This process will produce the first iteration of the Risk Register. The Risk Register should include the risk, cause and Triggers, Risk Owner, categories, and initial risk response. The initial iteration of the Risk Register will NOT include risk prioritization, analysis, Risk Scores, or detailed responses. Some key points to remember:

- Each risk should have a single Risk Owner. The Risk Owner will be validated and possibly changed during the Plan Risk Responses process. The Project Manager acts as the default Risk Owner if another Risk Team member is not identified. The Project Manager has an obligation to coach and train Risk Owners and encourage their participation.

- There is no limit to the number of risks identified. The more risks identified the better! However, as we'll discuss in the next chapter—all risks are not created equally!

- The Identify Risks process should include input from multiple stakeholders. Team members need to be included in the Identify Risks process as well. Creating a sense of ownership with the stakeholders responsible for managing risk is critical.

- The Risk Register serves as a key input for all Risk Management Process activities to follow. The Risk Register will be updated as the Risk Management Process progresses through the PIER-C process. Risk Register creation is an iterative process. You will continue to update the Risk Register as the project progresses. Version control is highly encouraged.

- PMI defines *Risk Metalanguage* as a method that enables the Project Manager to effectively identify and describe risks. Remember, the goal of the Identify Risks process is to identify as many negative and positive risks as possible.

  o Negative risks can impact time, cost, and scope in an adverse way.

o Positive risks, on the other hand, can compensate for negative risks and allow for improved time, cost, and scope performance.

o This three-step method to develop a risk statement is illustrated in Figure 3.1:

Figure 3.1 Risk Metalanguage

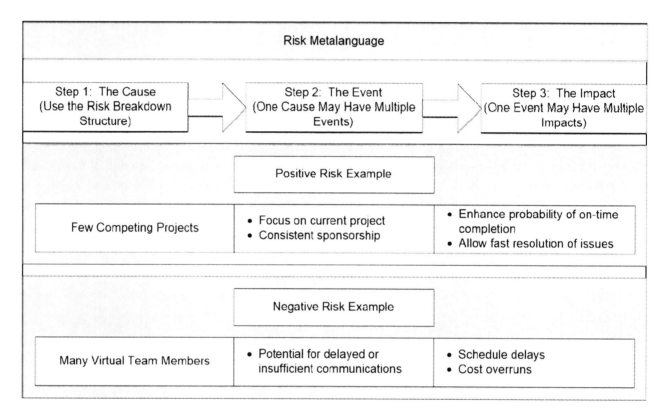

Identify Risks Process

The Identify Risks process consists of the inputs, tools and techniques, and output that are shown in Figure 3.2 below.

Figure 3.2 Identify Risks Process

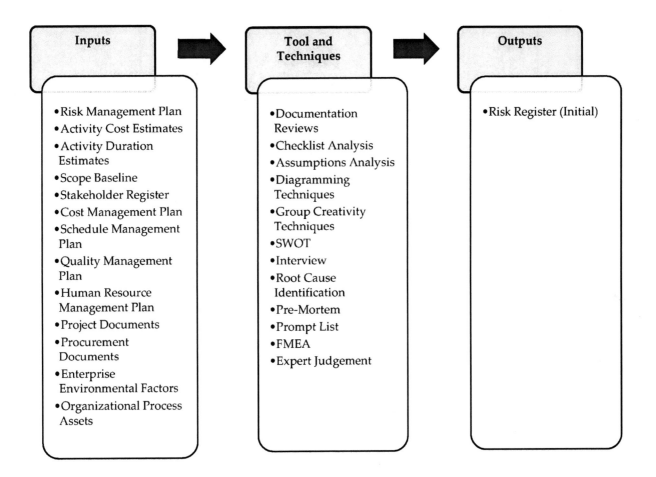

Inputs

- Risk Management Plan
- Activity Cost Estimates
- Activity Duration Estimates
- Scope Baseline
- Stakeholder Register
- Cost Management Plan
- Schedule Management Plan
- Quality Management Plan
- Human Resource Management Plan
- Project Documents
- Procurement Documents
- Enterprise Environmental Factors
- Organizational Process Assets

Tool and Techniques

- Documentation Reviews
- Checklist Analysis
- Assumptions Analysis
- Diagramming Techniques
- Group Creativity Techniques
- SWOT
- Interview
- Root Cause Identification
- Pre-Mortem
- Prompt List
- FMEA
- Expert Judgement

Outputs

- Risk Register (Initial)

Identify Risks: Inputs

A number of inputs should be available when beginning the Identify Risks process. A list of key inputs, along with their applicability, is below.

Input	Applicability
Risk Management Plan	Defines processes and strategy to accomplish end-to-end Project Risk Management. Defines methodology, roles, and availability of Resource Breakdown Structures.
Activity Cost Estimates	Where there are cost estimates, there is risk. Consider stakeholder tolerances and thresholds when costs are estimated.
Activity Duration Estimates	Where there are time duration estimates, there is risk. Consider stakeholder tolerances and thresholds.
Scope Baseline	Includes Scope Statement, WBS, and WBS Dictionary. Scope Statement lists assumptions. WBS defines activities at the summary, control account, or work package levels. WBS also defines the nature of a project as a first of its kind or recurring.
Stakeholder Register	Includes key information about stakeholders. Normally includes: • Identification Information • Assessment Information: Requirements, expectations, interest and influence factors • Classification: Internal/External. Supporter/Neutral, etc.
Cost Management Plan	Defines how risk budgets and Contingency/Management Reserves will be reported and assessed. Defines approach to cost management.
Schedule Management Plan	Defines how schedule contingencies will be reported and assessed. Defines approach to time management.
Quality Management Plan	Defines specific approach to quality. Includes metrics, targets, standards, checklist for Quality Control, process improvement, etc.
Human Resource Management Plan	Defines the organizational structure for the project. Delineates roles and responsibilities and provides a Staffing Management Plan.
Project Documents	Includes Assumption Log, Work Performance Reports, Earned Value Technique metrics, Network Diagrams, Baselines, etc.
Procurement Documents	Includes Statement of Work, source selection criteria, and appropriate procurement documents that will be used to develop agreements for seller support.
Enterprise Environmental Factors	Includes published information, studies, checklists, risk attitudes, benchmarking, and industry studies.
Organizational Process Assets	Includes project files, documented controls, Lessons Learned, templates, and other historical information.

Identify Risks: Tools and Techniques

Tools and techniques used in the Identify Risks process include looking at the past, present, and the future. Historical information allows a Project Manager to compare current projects with past projects. This information provides valuable information that can be used to identify risks, issues, and benefits. Creativity techniques help to identify future risks.

Testing Note: All tools and techniques used in the Identify Risks process fall into three categories. They include the past (Historical Reviews), the present (Current Assessments), and the future (Creativity Techniques).

- **Documentation Reviews**: Read through all project documentation. Is it clear? Is it understandable? Do documented methods match the goals of the project? Ensure documents are reviewed, edited, and clearly communicated to all stakeholders.

- **Checklist Analysis**: Lessons Learned allow for the development of checklists supporting a variety of project types. The Checklist Analysis approach identifies potential risks and helps plan for them ahead of time.

  o Checklist Analysis is a quick and simple approach used to perform an initial high-level analysis of risks. Checklist Analysis will not identify new risks that are not on the checklist. This is a limitation.

- **Assumptions Analysis**: Assumptions are risks waiting to happen. By virtue of their definition, "those factors thought to be true without certain proof," they are dangerous. Assumptions Analysis *needs* to occur on every project. All assumptions must be validated or dismissed through analysis and research.

- **Diagramming Techniques**: PMI shares some common diagramming methods that can be used for risk identification. Many of these techniques support the project Quality Management Process. They include:

  o *Cause and Effect Diagrams*: Each cause of a potential effect is a risk factor that should be considered. Alternate names for Cause and Effect Diagrams are Ishikawa Diagrams or Fishbone Diagrams.

o *System of Process Flow Charts*: Every Project Manager should learn how to map and analyze processes. Process flowcharts reveal how systems function and interrelate and serve as a superb means of identifying potential risks.

o *Influence Diagrams*: This method includes graphical representations of situations showing causal influences, time ordering of events, and other relationships among variables and outcomes.

- **Group Creativity Techniques**: PMI lists a number of potential methods for gathering information. A number of questions from this area appear on the exam. More importantly, these are tools and techniques that all managers need to understand and leverage on an everyday basis.

  o *Brainstorming*: *This technique is **both** an Information Gathering Technique and Group Creativity Technique per the PMBOK!* It's an open forum where members generate ideas and solve problems. A facilitator logs inputs. Brainstorming is one method used for attaining expert input. *Refrain from evaluating responses during the Brainstorming session.* This could impact the success of this Information Gathering session.

  o *Delphi Technique*: *This technique is **both** an Information Gathering Technique and Group Creativity Technique per the PMBOK!* Gain inputs and consensus through anonymous inputs. Reduces fear of reprisal. Delphi Technique is also a method used to attain expert input. Note the diagram for Delphi Technique at the end of this section.

    ▪ Surveys and questionnaires are two common methods used to solicit information.

    ▪ A key goal of Delphi Technique is to share the end results with all who participated. Sharing information allows the experts who participated to expand their knowledge base. In addition, feedback will likely be generated that assists in identifying more risks than initially identified.

    ▪ Delphi Technique is a tool that provides Social Intelligence. It reduces fear and intimidation factors. Delphi Technique is sometimes termed Social Intelligence.

o *Nominal Group Technique:* This technique is similar to Brainstorming. Input is collected from a select group. This input is analyzed and rank ordered by the group.

o *Affinity Diagramming*: This method uses the intellectual power of a group to place risks into categories. This is the *best method to use when it is believed that all possible risks were not identified.*

o *Idea/Mind Mapping:* Consolidate ideas through individual Brainstorming sessions into a single map to reflect commonality and differences in understanding and to generate new ideas.

- **SWOT:** Analyze opportunities and threats based on strengths and weaknesses. A diagram of SWOT is provided at the end of this section as well.

  o Strengths and weaknesses are internal. Opportunities and threats are external.

  o Strengths lead to opportunities or positive risks. Weaknesses lead to threats or negative risks.

- **Interview:** This is a one-on-one discussion with key stakeholders or experts in a given field. A drawback of this technique is that it takes time and is slow. *This is also an Information Gathering Technique.*

- **Root Cause Identification:** This is the same as Cause and Effect Analysis (synonymous with Ishikawa Diagramming and Fishbone Diagramming). *Grouping risks by common causes can aid in developing more effective risk responses. This is also an Information Gathering Technique.*

- **Pre-Mortem:** This is a method used to identify potential risks before a project begins. Review your project and compare it to past projects that were similar. Try to determine what could go right or wrong with your project before the project begins. Key sources of information that can be leveraged include expert input, historical records, Lessons Learned, etc.

- **Prompt List:** This is a generic list of categories where risks may be found. This list is used to "prompt" ideas and risk identification.

- **FMEA:** Failure Modes and Effect Analysis (FMEA) is a tool that identifies potential failure modes, determines effects of each failure, and seeks ways to mitigate the probability and impact of each failure.

- **Expert Judgement:** Identify risks as a team. Include all stakeholders in the process.

Tools and techniques applicable to the Identify Risks activity should be defined in the Project Risk Management Plan. In addition, roles, responsibilities, and key stakeholders who should participate in the Identify Risks activity should be defined, as well.

Identify Risks Process Tools and Techniques Visuals

Figure 3.3 Delphi Technique

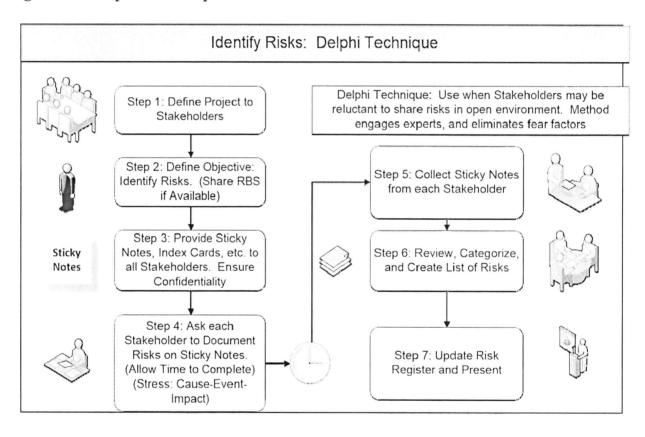

Figure 3.4 SWOT

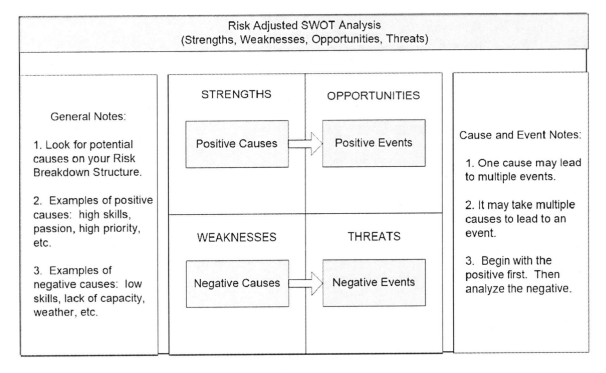

Identify Risks Output: Risk Register

The key output of the Identify Risks process is the *initial* Risk Register. This Risk Register will become a part of the formal Project Management Plan when approved and accepted and will become part of the Project Baseline.

Remember this key point: The initial Risk Register will be updated during the next stages in the project Risk Management Process. The Risk Register acts as an input for all Risk Management process steps that follow. In addition, remember that risk identification should be performed as early as possible in the project lifecycle. The earlier risks are identified, the quicker you can develop appropriate responses.

Figure 3.5 Initial Risk Register

Risk	Cause and Triggers	Risk Owner	Category	Risk Response
		Initial		Initial
The initial Risk Owner and Risk Response are defined during the Identify Risks process. This information will be revisited and validated during the Plan Risk Responses process.				

Testing Note: Remember the entries recommended for inclusion in the initial Risk Register. They include:

1. Definition of the Risk (Event and Consequence)

2. Causes and Triggers for the Individual Risk

3. Initial Risk Owner (this will be revisited and validated later)

4. Risk Categorization

5. Initial Risk Response (this will be revisited and validated later)

Identify Risks: Keys to Success

- *Timing*: Worth repeating! Risk identification should occur as early in the project as possible. Known risks can be analyzed and addressed. Unknown risks may catch stakeholders by surprise. Remember, manage risk, or it will manage you.

- *Frequency*: The Identify Risks process is a recurring or iterative process. Repeat the process periodically when it makes sense or adds value. This often depends upon situations within the project. Emergent Risks are waiting to be identified.

- *Sources*: Use multiple sources to find and identify risks—the more sources, the better. In addition, solicit inputs from multiple stakeholders to obtain multiple perspectives.

- *New Risk Validation*: Always ask for as much information as needed to clearly define any new risks reported. Always share new risks with as many stakeholders as needed in an effort to learn as much as possible about the cause, risk, and effects.

- *Risk Statements:* Remember that the best risk definition uses the risk metalanguage methodology of Cause-Risk-Effect. Goals are to achieve the proper level of detail and reduce ambiguity.

- *Link Risks to Objectives*: Remember that each risk should have the potential to impact a key project objective (scope, time, cost, quality). Do not list a risk that does not impact a project objective.

- *Risk Types:* Remember to identify both positive risks and negative risks. We tend to key on the negatives and often forget to identify the positives. Avoid lost opportunities!

- *Ownership:* Initial Risk Owners are assigned during the Identify Risks process. Remember that each risk should have a specific owner. There should only be one Risk Owner for each risk. Every risk response that is agreed to and funded must have a Risk Owner.

- *Visibility*: The Risk Register needs to be made available to all project stakeholders for review. In addition, the Risk Register should be used as a primary tool to review risks at periodic project status meetings.

Activity 3: Identify Risks Process Review

Directions: Respond to the twelve true or false questions below. Answers are in Appendix A.

Question	True or False
1. The Identify Risks process produces the final iteration of the Risk Register.	
2. Checklist Analysis is a fast and efficient means of identifying new risks missed during the initial review.	
3. Another term for Delphi Technique is Social Intelligence. It allows experts to review the final results and provide additional feedback.	
4. SWOT analysis is a practical means to gather information from a group of selected stakeholders and rank order the inputs.	
5. The Stakeholder Register provides a strategy for managing stakeholder expectations.	
6. The worst thing to do during a Brainstorming session is to evaluate participant responses.	
7. The Risk Register should have restricted access and not be made available to all project stakeholders.	
8. The Risk Register is an essential input that will allow for development of a comprehensive Risk Management Plan.	
9. Roles and responsibilities supporting the Identify Risks process are defined during the Plan Risk Management process.	
10. Emergent Risks should be added to the Risk Register.	
11. It is best to identify risks at the conclusion of all other project planning activities.	
12. Identify Risks process tools and techniques include tools that look into the past, present, and future.	

Chapter 4: Perform Qualitative Risk Analysis Process

Process 3: Perform Qualitative Risk Analysis

Perform Qualitative Risk Analysis is the third process in Project Risk Management. The focus of this process is to prioritize risks for further actions. Qualitative Risk Analysis results are *subjective.* This analysis uses the Risk Management Plan and Risk Register to assess *probability and impact* for each risk.

- The ultimate goal of the Perform Qualitative Risk Analysis process is to update the initial Risk Register.

- Outputs of Qualitative Risk Analysis can lead to a Go/No Go decision. It may be determined that a project is too risky to pursue as a result of this process.

- Considering causes of risk when calculating probability and impact is helpful during this step. It is not uncommon for a single cause to result in multiple potential events and effects/consequences.

- *Path Convergence* is a prioritization consideration as well. Path convergence is defined as multiple activities flowing into or from a central activity.

    o The *Project Network Diagram* shows dependencies for all activities and identifies where paths converge. In the figure below, multiple activities flow from Activity A. Greater levels of path convergence increase risk probability and impact.

    o Refer to Figure 4.1. Activities B, C, and D are dependent upon completion of Activity A. A risk that impacts Activity A potentially has a greater impact to the project.

Figure 4.1 Path Convergence Model

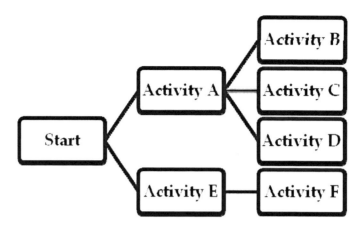

Perform Qualitative Risk Analysis Process

The Perform Qualitative Risk Analysis process consists of the inputs, tools and techniques, and outputs shown in Figure 4.2 below.

Figure 4.2 Perform Qualitative Risk Analysis Process

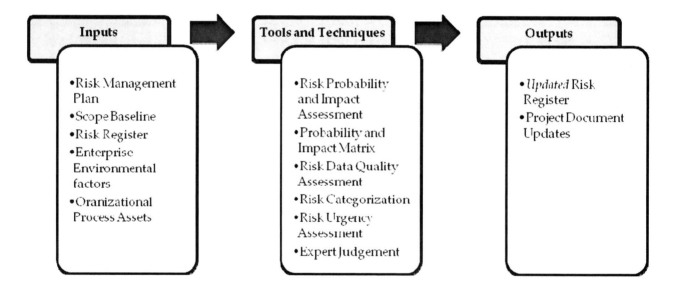

Perform Qualitative Risk Analysis: Inputs

Outputs from the two previous risk management processes are key inputs to the Perform Qualitative Risk Analysis process. These are the Risk Management Plan and Risk Register. Note the hard dependency. This process is dependent upon completion of the prior two.

Input	Applicability
Risk Management Plan	Defines roles, responsibilities and methodologies to evaluate risks. *Also provides definitions for probability and impact that are the core of this process.*
Risk Register	Provides the initial list of risks to be evaluated. The Risk Register will be updated during this process.
Scope Baseline	Includes the Scope Statement, Work Breakdown Structure (WBS) and WBS Dictionary.
Enterprise Environmental Factors	May include industry studies of similar projects by risk specialists or risk databases from industry or proprietary sources.
Organizational Process Assets	Includes risk databases, historical information, studies of previous projects, templates, Lessons Learned, etc. May include Risk Rating rules.

Perform Qualitative Risk Analysis: Tools and Techniques

Tools and techniques are designed to help achieve the final result of the Perform Qualitative Risk Analysis process. The Perform Qualitative Risk Analysis process is a fast and effective method to prioritize risks on the Risk Register for further action as necessary.

- **Risk Probability and Impact Assessment**: All risks should be evaluated and scored for probability (also called *likelihood*) and impact (also called *consequence* or *effect*). A consistent scoring system for all risks should be used. Remember that the values for probability and risk should be defined in the Risk Management Plan.

   o *Probability*: Probability is the potential for a risk to occur. Scoring systems include percentages, or a numeric scale (1-5 for example). The assigned score is called a *Risk Rating*. If a Risk Rating is too high, try to find ways to eliminate the cause. This method is called avoidance.

o *Impact*: Impact is defined as the consequences the risk event will have on the project. Impact should be linked to project objectives. Remember that primary project objectives are scope, time, cost, and quality. Scoring can be based on many factors specific to the project. It is not uncommon to use weighted impact ratings that may assign higher values to higher impact risks. For example, if schedule is the number one project priority, rate risks impacting schedule higher than others. The numeric score used for impact is also called a Risk Rating.

o Multiply the Probability Risk Rating × the Impact Risk Rating to calculate a Risk Score. The Risk Score may determine whether or not risk responses are developed. The Risk Score also dictates the level of detail responses should have. Higher Risk Scores dictate higher levels of response detail and vice-versa. See Figure 4.3 below. Risk A has the highest priority based on achieving the highest Risk Score. Risk D is the lowest priority risk, despite having the highest impact score.

Figure 4.3 Calculating a Risk Score

Risk	Probability Risk Rating	Impact Risk Rating	Risk Score
A	4	4	16
B	3	4	12
C	2	4	8
D	1	5	5

- **Probability and Impact Matrix:** Many organizations develop a standard Probability and Risk Matrix that shows Risk Ratings and overall priority determinations. A Probability and Impact Risk Matrix can be simple or elaborate depending upon the prioritization methodology you select.

o This tool is sometimes referred to as a *Lookup Table.*

o Focusing on high priority risks is the best means to improve overall project performance.

o Remember this key concept: Describing your Risk Rating criteria and developing a Probability and Impact Matrix reduces potential for bias and improves overall analysis. The Probability and Impact Matrix is part of the Risk Management Plan.

o Figure 4.4 shows an example of a simple Probability and Impact Matrix.

Figure 4.4 Probability and Impact Matrix Example

Probability and Impact Scoring	Low Probability	Moderate Probability	High Probability
Low Impact	1	2	3
Moderate Impact	2	4	6
High Impact	3	6	9
Place all risks with score of 4 or below on Watch List Develop responses for all risks with score of 6 or higher			

- **Risk Data Quality Assessment:** Review data used to determine Probability and Impact Scores to ensure it is accurate and unbiased. Data used may not be sufficient to accurately define a Risk Score (Probability × Impact). If this is the case, annotate the risk as requiring further information to improve understanding before final analysis can be complete. *In addition, always correct a risk assessment that was impacted by bias.*

  o **Note**: Some Probability and Impact Scoring uses Heuristics. This is any approach to problem solving, learning, or discovery that employs a practical method not guaranteed to be optimal or perfect, but sufficient for the immediate goals. Where finding an optimal solution is impossible or impractical, heuristic methods can be used to speed up the process of finding a satisfactory solution. Heuristics can be mental shortcuts that ease the cognitive load of making a decision. Heuristics models are sometimes referred to as "Rules of Thumb."

- Types of bias that should be understood, as well as some concepts impacting bias include:

  o *Motivational Bias*: This occurs when stakeholders intentionally try to bias ratings one way or another.

  o *Cognitive Bias:* This is bias based on perceptions. It is said, "Perception is reality."

- *Bias may be desired.* It may be desirable to create bias toward high priority risks. For example, if schedule is the number one priority, rules that rate schedule risks higher than other types or categories should be established and implemented.

- The best way to reduce bias during the Perform Qualitative Risk Analysis process is to define levels for Probability and Impact and provide a Probability and Impact Matrix to reduce subjectivity of results.

- **Risk Categorization:** *Grouping risks by category assists in defining better risk responses* as the Risk Management Process moves forward. This practice also allows for a determination of common causes that impact multiple risks.

- **Risk Urgency Assessment**: The desired output of the Perform Qualitative Risk Analysis process is a prioritized list of risks. A number of questions need responses. Which risks must be addressed immediately? Which risks can be placed on a Watch List as low priority? A risk urgency assessment prioritizes your risk response activities.

  - Risks requiring an immediate response are placed on an Urgent List. The Risk Rating determines the level of urgency. Risks may be listed separately based on scope, time, cost, or quality objectives.

  - Risks that do not require immediate responses based on low Risk Score are placed on the Watch List. In essence, these risks are accepted in the near term. Responses will only be developed if Risk Score increases.

Perform Qualitative Risk Analysis: Additional Tools and Techniques

- **Pareto Prioritization Analysis**: Pareto Charts track problems or issues from most to least. *The idea is that 20% of all causes result in 80% of all effects.* Pareto Charts can be helpful in determining Probability Scores. Problems occurring with the greatest frequency warrant a higher Probability Score. An example is provided in Figure 4.5.

Figure 4.5 Pareto Chart Example

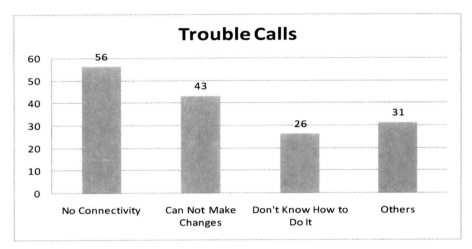

Trouble Calls

- **Root Cause Analysis:** This tool as shown in Figure 4.6 is used to determine root causes of problems. It is sometimes called a Fishbone Diagram or Ishikawa Diagram. Causes that potentially have the greatest impact should warrant a higher impact score.

Figure 4.6 Root Cause Analysis Example

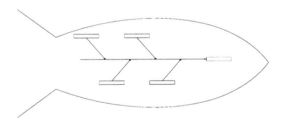

- **Risk Breakdown Structure Analysis:** We introduced the Risk Breakdown Structure as a tool you can use to identify risks. Some organizations expand the Risk Breakdown Structure to add a probability factor. Most scales use a high, moderate to high, moderate, low to moderate, or low frequency rating. This conforms well to traditional 1 through 5 Likert scales, which are quite common.

- **Risk Scores:** Some organizations total all risks. In the example below, there are four risks for a hypothetical project. Three risks are negative and one is positive. Note the scoring.

o   Three negative risks total 25 points (12 + 8 + 5 = 25)

o   One positive risk totals 16 points. This number is subtracted from the 25 score to provide a total Risk Score of 9.

o   The Goal: Reduce negative Risk Scores through effective risk management techniques. Increase positive Risk Scores. In the end, the lower the Risk Score, the greater chance of project success.

o   **Risk Metric Trend Analysis:** Trending Risk Scores as a project progresses is a best practice. If a project's overall Risk Score is increasing, this is a red flag. On the other hand, if total Risk Score is decreasing, then this is great news. Use Risk Trend Analysis to show stakeholders that the project risk management methods are working, or as a means to share that a project is in trouble.

Perform Qualitative Risk Analysis Output: Update the Risk Register

The project Risk Register is updated at the conclusion of the Perform Qualitative Risk Analysis process. Potential updates may include, but are not limited to:

- Ranking or prioritizing risks: Risk Ratings for all risks should be added to the Risk Register. Each Probability Risk and Impact Risk is assigned a numeric score, or Risk Rating. Multiply the Probability and Impact Risk Ratings to calculate a Risk Score.

- Project Risk Score: Add all individual Risk Scores to calculate the Project Risk Score. Risk Exposure is a term that defines the level of risk on a project. The Project Risk Score determines Risk Exposure. Acceptable levels of Risk Exposure are based on stakeholder attitudes, tolerances, and thresholds.

  o   Example: Project A has a Risk Score of 113. Acceptable levels of Risk Exposure may be defined as projects with Risk Exposure of less than 90. In this case, the Project Manager needs to take action to lower the Risk Score. If this is not possible, the Risk Score may lead to a Go/No Go decision for the project.

- Grouping by risk category: Validate the categorization completed during the Identify Risks process.

- Risks requiring near-term responses: These are risks on the Urgent List. The higher the Risk Score, the more urgent the risk.

- Risks requiring additional analysis: Additional information may be necessary to score certain risks. Mark these risks for further analysis.

- Watch Lists of low priority risks: The Project Manager is the primary owner of risks on the Watch List.

- Risk trends—Example: Are more risks developing in a particular category?

Figure 4.7 shows how the Risk Register evolves at the completion of the Perform Qualitative Risk Analysis process. Note that key terms and concepts are underlined and in *italics* on this example. A number of updates are applied to the Risk Register at the end of this step.

Figure 4.7 Updated Risk Register Example

Risk	Cause	Risk Owner	Category	Risk Response	Probability *Risk Rating*	Impact *Risk Rating*	*Risk Score*
		Initial		Initial	Add in Step 3	Add in Step 3	Add in Step 3
This is the Urgent List for high priority risks.							
							Risk Rating within project: Shows how individual Risk Score compares with other Risk Scores.
Draw the line on the Risk Register at the conclusion of the Perform Qualitative Risk Analysis process. Risks that are high priority fall on the Urgent List, and responses are developed. Low priority risks are placed on the Watch List. Responses are developed if the Risk Score increases.							
This is the Watch List for low priority risks.							
							Project Risk Score = Total of all Risk Scores

Note 1: Step 3 is the Perform Qualitative Risk Analysis process.

Note 2: The entries in this example are the basic Risk Register entries recommended by PMI. An actual Risk Register is not restricted to these entries. Remember that the Project Manager determines what needs to be represented on the Risk Register. Do, however, remember these entries and this format for test-taking purposes.

Note 3: Interviews and meetings are the two most effective means to complete the Perform Qualitative Risk Analysis process.

Perform Qualitative Risk Analysis: Keys to Success

- *Probability and Impact Scoring*: Probability and Impact Scoring criteria are listed in the Risk Management Plan. Scoring systems should be approved and accepted by all stakeholders. Pre-determined scoring systems may be included in Organizational Process Assets in the form of a Probability and Impact Matrix.

  o Define Probability and Impact criteria in the Risk Management Plan. For example, if scoring Probability on a 1 to 5 scale, what factors would constitute a score of four? This practice eliminates bias and improves the quality of your analysis.

  o Here is a scenario to remember. A risk was initially identified for a twelve month project to have a probability of 20%. The project is now in its seventh month. What is the probability the risk will occur? **Hint**: Do not overanalyze this scenario. If there is no new information, nothing changed. The 20% probability in month one is still a 20% probability in month seven!

- *Urgency*: Urgency levels should be documented and agreed upon. Create some type of Probability and Impact Matrix that allows prioritization based on score. Some organizations have a standard Probability and Impact Matrix available as part of Organizational Process Assets. The matrix does not need to be elaborate. Here is a second example of a Probability and Impact Matrix in simpler form.

Figure 4.8 Simplified Probability and Impact Matrix

Low Priority Score	Moderate Priority Score	High Priority Score
8 or below.	9-12	13 to 25

- *Quality Data*: Qualitative Risk Analysis is subjective. It is important to ensure data used to make probability × impact scoring decisions is of the highest quality and reliability.

- *Frequency:* Perform Qualitative Risk Analysis is an iterative process. Guidelines should be defined in the Risk Management Plan. Remember that the Perform Qualitative Risk Analysis process is always performed. If a new risk is identified, then the Perform Qualitative Risk Analysis process is your next step.

- *Bias*: It is important to reduce cognitive and motivational bias as defined earlier. Try to find unbiased sources to help score risks as accurately as possible. Qualitative Risk Analysis requires accurate and unbiased data if it is to be credible.

Activity 4: Perform Qualitative Risk Analysis

Directions: There are a number of key definitions and concepts you need to understand. Match the definition or scenario to the potential responses provided. Answers are in Appendix A.

Perform Qualitative Risk Analysis Definition and Concept Activity	Response
1. The product of multiplying probability times impact.	
2. A situation where multiple activities feed into a single activity. Increases risk.	
3. A numeric value that shows how an individual Risk Score compares with other individual Risk Scores.	
4. The chances that a risk event may occur.	
5. A list of risks determined to be very high priority.	
6. Term that defines the level of risk on a project as defined by the Project Risk Score.	
7. Situation where stakeholder Risk Ratings and Risk Scores are impacted by perceptions.	
8. The two most effective ways to accomplish the Perform Qualitative Risk Analysis process.	
9. The cumulative value of all Risk Scores.	
10. A key planning tool that must be updated at the completion of the Perform Qualitative Risk Analysis process.	
11. A key input that facilitates performance of the Perform Qualitative Risk Analysis process.	
12. Situation occurs when stakeholders intentionally try to manipulate and impact Risk Ratings and Risk Scores.	
13. A list of risks determined to be a lower priority than others.	

14. The numeric values assigned to show the probability and impact of a risk event.	
15. Standard Probability and Risk Matrix that shows ratings and overall priority determinations.	
16. A numeric Risk Rating that expresses the consequences to a project if a risk occurs.	

Activity 4: Choose from the following:

A. Path Convergence

B. Meetings and Interviews

C. Watch List

D. Urgent List

E. Risk Exposure

F. Risk Rating

G. Project Risk Score

H. Risk Score

I. Risk Rating within Project

J. Motivational Bias

K. Cognitive Bias

L. Lookup Table

M. Probability

N. Impact

O. Risk Register

P. Scope Baseline

Chapter 5: Perform Quantitative Risk Analysis

Process 4: Perform Quantitative Risk Analysis

Perform Quantitative Risk Analysis is the fourth process in Project Risk Management and keys on *numerical analysis*. The Perform Quantitative Risk Analysis process uses the updated Risk Register from the Perform Qualitative Risk Analysis process and provides an *objective* analysis of risk factors and the potential to impact a project.

Here are specific objectives of the Quantitative Risk Analysis process, as defined in the *PMBOK*:

- Quantify possible project outcomes and probabilities. The Quantitative Risk Analysis process considers the *impact of multiple risks on desired project objectives or outcomes simultaneously*. This process analyzes the effects of risk that may substantially impact the project's competing demands.

- Analyze Pessimistic, Most Likely, and Optimistic scenarios using Three Point Estimating methods. (Includes Program Evaluation Review Technique, or PERT.)

- Assess the probability of achieving specific project objectives. Tools such as Monte Carlo, which provides specific timeframes or points when risk potential is highest, or Standard Deviation Analysis are quite effective for simulating probabilities of response.

- Identify risks requiring the most attention by quantifying their relative contribution to overall project risk.

- Identify realistic and achievable cost, schedule, scope, and quality targets in light of risk. *Determine Contingency Reserves required* for responses to risks.

- Determine the best project management decision when some conditions or outcomes are uncertain. Make decisions based on objective, rather than subjective data.

<u>Note</u>: While the Perform Quantitative Risk Analysis process is not always accomplished, the Perform Qualitative Risk Analysis process is always mandatory. Considerations to perform the Quantitative Risk Analysis process include:

- Cost, length, or relative priority of the project.

- Time and effort required versus benefits to be received.

- Complexity of the project and decisions to make a Go/No Go decision.

Perform Quantitative Risk Analysis Process

The Perform Quantitative Risk Analysis process consists of inputs, tools and techniques, and outputs shown in Figure 5.1 below.

Figure 5.1 Perform Quantitative Risk Analysis Process

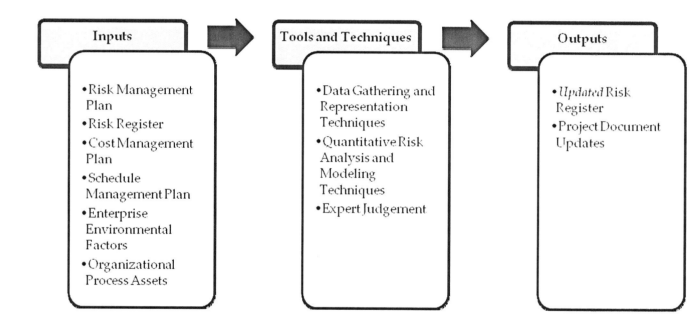

Inputs
- Risk Management Plan
- Risk Register
- Cost Management Plan
- Schedule Management Plan
- Enterprise Environmental Factors
- Organizational Process Assets

Tools and Techniques
- Data Gathering and Representation Techniques
- Quantitative Risk Analysis and Modeling Techniques
- Expert Judgement

Outputs
- Updated Risk Register
- Project Document Updates

Perform Quantitative Risk Analysis: Inputs

A number of inputs are required to successfully complete the Perform Qualitative Risk Analysis process.

Input	Applicability
Risk Management Plan	Defines roles and responsibilities and methodologies to evaluate risks.
Risk Register	Provides the initial list of risks to be evaluated. The Risk Register will be updated during this process.
Cost Management Plan	Sets format and criteria for planning, structuring, estimating, budgeting, and controlling project costs. Controls help establish approach to the Quantitative Risk Analysis process of the budget or cost plan.
Schedule Management Plan	Sets format and criteria for developing and controlling the project schedule. Controls and nature of the schedule itself will help structure an approach to the Quantitative Risk Analysis process of the schedule.
Enterprise Environmental Factors	Culture, values, and systems. May include industry studies of similar projects, risk databases, etc.
Organizational Process Assets	Includes risk databases, historical information, studies of previous projects, templates, Lessons Learned, etc. May include Risk Rating rules.

Perform Quantitative Risk Analysis: Tools and Techniques

PMI divides tools and techniques into two broad categories.

Data Gathering and Representation Techniques

- **Interviewing**: Interviewing expert stakeholders is a common method used to determine risk impact. Generally, interviews are used to determine optimistic, most likely, and pessimistic scenarios for time and cost estimates. These estimates are used when estimating using Three Point Estimating methods, such as PERT.

  o Try to include a mix of open-ended and prepared questions when conducting interviews. Begin with open-ended questions to gain insight from the interviewer. Follow up with prepared questions.

o Remember interviewing takes more time than other tools and techniques. It takes time to conduct interviews with each individual stakeholder.

- **Probability Distributions**: Probability distribution estimates the potential of a risk event to occur over a pre-described range. A number of distribution types impact risk management.

   o *Normal Distributions*: Estimating using Three Point methods assume a normal distribution. The normal distribution curve is also referred to as the Bell Curve. A normal distribution model uses averages and Sigma intervals to show the potential range of values over the length of the curve. See Figure 5.2 for an example.

Figure 5.2 Normal Distribution Curve

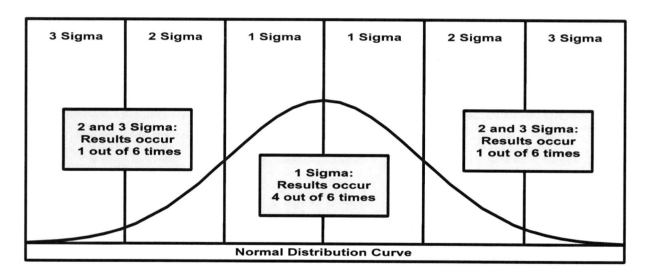

o The higher the Standard Deviation, the greater the risk. Standard Deviation is a numeric indicator that helps calculate the range of potential results. It represents the distance we travel from the mean as we extend across a normal distribution. The greater the range, the greater the risk. Using Figure 5.3 as an example, let's assume a mean of 20. See how the range changes in the table below when we compare a Standard Deviation of 2 to a Standard Deviation of 3.

Figure 5.3 Standard Deviation Illustration

Optimistic			Most Likely	Pessimistic		
Sigma 3	Sigma 2	Sigma 1	Mean	Sigma 1	Sigma 2	Sigma 3
14	16	18	20 (SD=2)	22	24	26
11	14	17	20 (SD=3)	23	26	29

- o The following represents the percentage of returns that fall within each Sigma range assuming a normal distribution or Bell Curve.

  - **1 Sigma:** Results occur within 1 Sigma 68.26% of the time. In estimating, we assume returns fall within 1 Sigma of the mean 4 out of 6 times. In the example above, results using a Standard Deviation of 2 range from 18 to 22 at 1 Sigma. The range of 1 Sigma results increase from 17 to 23 when the Standard Deviation is changed to 3. This is a greater range of results which increases overall risk of achieving objectives.

  - **2 Sigma:** Results occur within 2 Sigma 95.46% of the time. In the example above, results using a Standard Deviation of 2 are 16 to 24 at 2 Sigma. The range in 2 Sigma increases from 14 to 26 when Standard Deviation is increased to 3. Risk increases as the Standard Deviation increases.

  - **3 Sigma:** Results occur within 3 Sigma 99.73% of the time. In estimating, we assume returns fall within the 2 Sigma and 3 Sigma range on each side of the mean one out of six times. In the example above, results using a Standard Deviation of 2 ranges from 14 to 26 at 3 Sigma. However, the range increases from 11 to 29 when the Standard Deviation is increased to 3 Sigma. Risk increases even more.

  - **6 Sigma:** Equals 99.99985 (3.4 defects per million). Know this value for test-taking purposes.

- *Uniform Distributions* are used in the Perform Quantitative Risk Analysis process as well. Risk is normally uniform in the early design stages of a project. Distribution becomes non-uniform in the later stages. Here is an illustration of a uniform distribution model.

Figure 5.4 Uniform Distribution Example

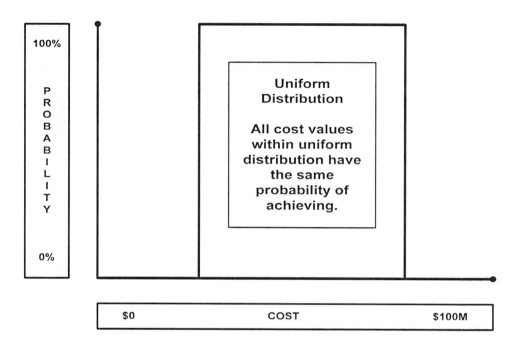

- *Triangular Distributions* illustrate where probability peaks at the mean. There is a fast decrease in probability as results move away from the mean. See Figure 5.5 for an example.

Figure 5.5 Triangular Distribution Example

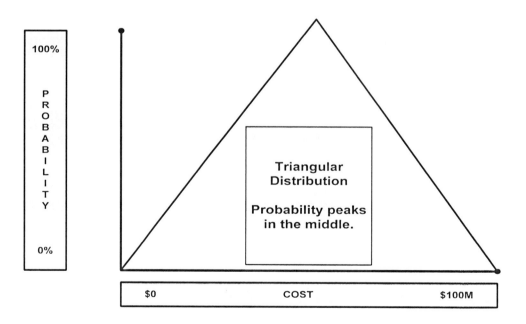

- *Beta Distributions* show where probability peaks on either side of the mean. See Figure 5.6 for an example.

Figure 5.6 Beta Distribution Example

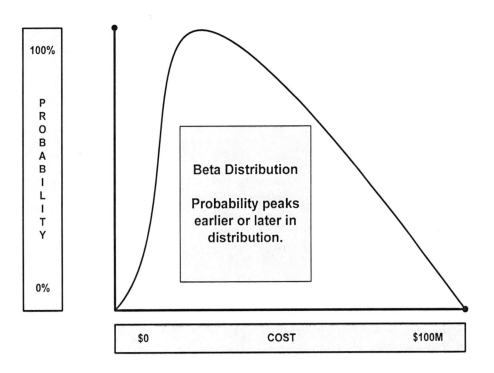

- **Three Point Estimating and PERT**: Three Point Estimating uses the Optimistic, Most Likely, and Pessimistic vales provided by experts to determine the best estimate. Figure 5.7 illustrates this concept.

Figure 5.7 Three Point Estimating and PERT

Estimate to Complete Activity	Number of Days Estimated
Optimistic	5 Days
Most Likely	10 Days
Pessimistic	21 Days

o **Three Point Averaging** takes the three estimates and averages them to determine the best estimate. Using the example above, add 5 + 10 + 21 = 36. Divide by 3 to determine the average (36/3 = 12). The best estimate equals 12 days. This is the default method on the PMI-RMP certification test.

o **PERT**: A second iteration of Three Point Estimating is a weighted average using PERT. PERT assumes results fall within a standard distribution. The formula for calculating an estimate using PERT is shown in Figure 5.8 below.

Figure 5.8 Calculating PERT

$$\frac{Pessimistic + (4 \times Most\ Likely) + Optimistic}{6}$$

Calculate by substituting the values in the example provided:

$$\frac{(21 + (4 \times 10) + 5)}{6} = 66/6 = 11\ Days\ for\ the\ estimate$$

o **Standard Deviation**: Standard Deviation can be calculated using optimistic, most likely, and pessimistic values. The formula is shown in Figure 5.9 below.

Figure 5.9 Calculating Standard Deviation

$$\frac{Pessimistic - Optimistic}{6}$$

Calculate by substituting the values in the example provided:

$$\frac{21\ Days - 5\ Days}{6} = 16/6 = 2.67\ Standard\ Deviation$$

Note: You may be asked to calculate Variance, which is calculated by squaring the Standard Deviation. For example, if Standard Deviation is 3, then Variance is 3 × 3 = 9.

Quantitative Risk Analysis and Modeling Techniques

- **Sensitivity Analysis:** Sensitivity Analysis uses several what if scenarios to calculate potential results. Sensitivity Analysis is a modeling technique that helps determine which risks have the greatest impact on a project. Sensitivity Analysis and What If Scenario Analysis both use Monte Carlo as a tool and technique.

  o Monte Carlo uses optimistic, most likely, and pessimistic estimates to determine the probability of meeting cost and/or schedule objectives.

  o A *Tornado Diagram* is generally the result of Sensitivity Analysis. A Tornado Diagram shows a single factor such as Net Present Value (NPV). It then visually displays variables that can impact the single variable. Here is an example in Figure 5.10.

Figure 5.10 Tornado Diagram Example

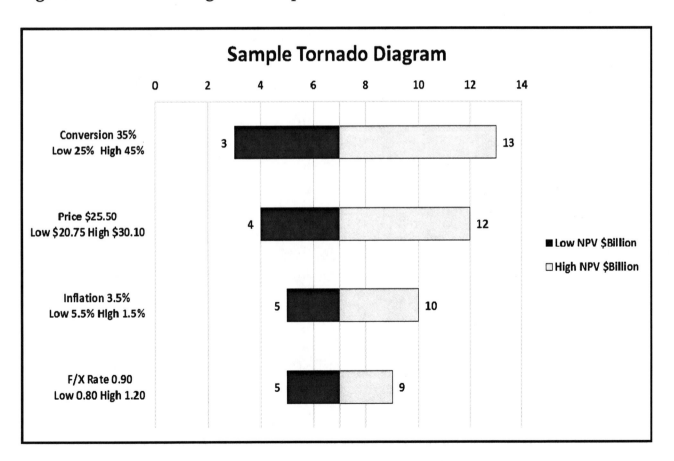

- *Monte Carlo*: Monte Carlo simulation is a computerized mathematical technique that allows people to account for risk in quantitative analysis and decision making. The technique is used by professionals in such widely disparate fields as finance, project management, energy, manufacturing, engineering, research and development, insurance, oil and gas, transportation, and the environment.[8]

  o *Monte Carlo simulation furnishes the decision maker with a range of possible outcomes and the probabilities they will occur for any choice of action.* It shows the extreme possibilities—the outcomes of going for broke and for the most conservative decision, along with all possible consequences for middle-of-the-road decisions.

  o The technique was first used by scientists working on the atom bomb; it was named for Monte Carlo, the Monaco resort town renowned for its casinos. Since its introduction in World War II, Monte Carlo simulation has been used to model a variety of physical and conceptual systems.

  o Monte Carlo simulation performs risk analysis by building models of possible results by substituting a range of values—a probability distribution—for any factor that has inherent uncertainty. It then calculates results over and over, each time using a different set of random values from the probability functions. Depending upon the number of uncertainties and the ranges specified for them, a Monte Carlo simulation could involve thousands or tens of thousands of recalculations before it is complete. Monte Carlo simulation produces distributions of possible outcome values.

  o By using probability distributions, variables can have different probabilities of different outcomes occurring. Probability distributions are a much more realistic way of describing uncertainty in variables of a risk analysis. Common probability distributions include:

    - **Normal** – Or Bell Curve. The user simply defines the mean or expected value and a standard deviation to describe the variation about the mean. Values in the middle near the mean are most likely to occur. It is symmetric and describes many natural phenomena, such as people's heights.

---

[8] Wikipedia

- **Lognormal** – Values are positively skewed, not symmetric like a normal distribution. It is used to represent values that don't go below zero but have unlimited positive potential.

- **Uniform** – All values have an equal chance of occurring, and the user simply defines the minimum and maximum.

- **Triangular** – The user defines the minimum, most likely, and maximum values. Values around the most likely are more likely to occur.

- **PERT**- The user defines the minimum, most likely, and maximum values, just like the triangular distribution. Values around the most likely are more likely to occur. However values between the most likely and extremes are more likely to occur than the triangular; that is, the extremes are not as emphasized.

- **Discrete** – The user defines specific values that may occur and the likelihood of each. An example might be: 20% chance of positive results, 30% change of negative results, and 50% chance average results.

o During a Monte Carlo simulation, values are sampled at random from the input probability distributions. Each set of samples is called an iteration, and the resulting outcome from that sample is recorded. Monte Carlo simulation does this hundreds or thousands of times, and the result is a probability distribution of possible outcomes. In this way, Monte Carlo simulation provides a much more comprehensive view of what may happen. It tells you not only what could happen, but how likely it is to happen.

Figure 5.11 provides a visual of Monte Carlo.

Figure 5.11 Monte Carlo Illustration

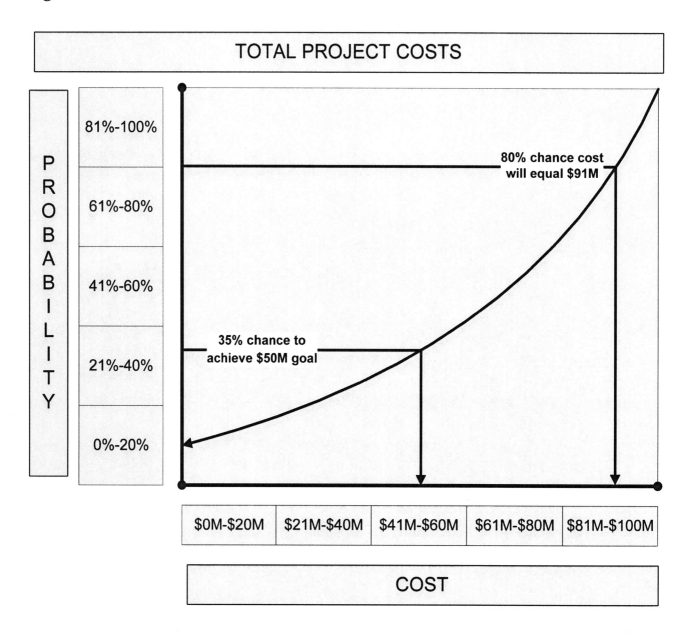

- **Expected Monetary Value (EMV)**: This is a method used widely to establish Contingency Reserve requirements for both budget and schedule. EMV is quantified by *multiplying probability times the best or worst case cost/time scenario.* Recall that risk can be positive or negative, and EMV provides the Expected Monetary Value of risk. Here is a sample scenario to illustrate EMV.

  o Four risks impact Project XYZ. They are risks A, B, C, and D.

- Risk A has a 30% chance of occurring and will cost the project $40,000. This is a negative risk. Using EMV, calculate the required Contingency Reserves for risk A as (.3 × $40,000 = $12,000). Add this amount to the project budget.

- Risk B has a 40% chance of occurring and will save the project ($10,000). (Numbers in parenthesis indicate a positive risk. Dollars are subtracted from your overall Contingency Reserve totals). This is a positive risk. Calculate (.4 × $10,000 = $4000). Subtract this amount from the project budget.

- Risk C has 75% chance of occurring and will cost the project $60,000. This is a negative risk. Calculate (.75 × $60,000 = $45,000). Add this amount.

- Risk D has a 50% chance of occurring and will cost the project $30,000. Calculate (.5 × $30,000 = $15,000). Add this amount.

How much in Contingency Reserves is needed for this project? Add up all negative and positive risk EMV totals. Total Contingency Reserve requirements equal $68,000 .

Figure 5.12 EMV Illustration

Risk	Probability	Maximum Dollar Impact of Risk	Contingency $ Required
A	30%	$40,000	$12,000
B	40%	($10,000)	($4,000)
C	75%	$60,000	$45,000
D	50%	$30,000	$15,000
Total	We add $68,000 to our project budget for Contingency Reserve needs.		$68,000

o Here is a variation to the previous scenario. If Risk D occurs, how much is left in Contingency Reserves? The project started with $68,000 in Contingency Reserves. A total of $30,000 was required to pay for negative Risk D. There is now $38,000 remaining in Contingency Reserves.

o Here is a second variation. If Risk B occurs, how much is left in the contingency fund? The project started with $68,000 in Contingency Reserves. The project gained $10,000 from positive Risk B. There is now $78,000 remaining in Contingency Reserves after this credit is added.

- **Decision Tree Analysis:** Decision Tree Analysis describes a scenario under consideration and uses available data to determine the most economic approach. The primary objective of Decision Tree Analysis is selecting the scenario that provides the best overall EMV. This is the highest EMV return, or lowest EMV costs. It should be noted that Decision Tree Analysis is considered as the most effective tool for development of appropriate risk responses.

    The following are some basic EMV scenarios:

    o Return + Return: A project has a fixed return of $100,000. There is a 20% chance of additional returns of $50,000 if the project finishes ahead of schedule. What is the value?

    - ($100,000 + (.2 × $50,000)) = ($100,000 + $10,000) = $110,000.

    o Return – Cost: A project has a guaranteed return of $200,000. There is a 40% chance that returns will be reduced by $80,000 due to cost overruns. What is the revised return projection?

    - ($200,000 – (.4 × $80,000)) = ($200,000 – $32,000) = $168,000.

    o Cost + Cost: A project has a set cost of $60,000. There is a 60% chance of incurring additional costs of $40,000 due to shipping delays. What is the total cost estimate?

    - ($60,000 + (.6 × $40,000)) = ($60,000 + $24,000) = $84,000.

    o Comparisons: Two scenarios may be presented on the exam. Always choose the option with the lowest costs or highest returns.

    o A Decision Tree Diagram may be presented. Test takers will be asked to analyze the scenarios presented, and choose the option providing highest returns or lowest costs. The following example illustrates a "make or buy" decision. The make value is $17M. The buy value is $32M. In this case, you choose the buy scenario.

    - Make Decision: (.3 × $180M) + (.7 × $90M) – $100M = $17M

- Buy Decision: (.3 × $120M) + (.7 × $80M) — $60M = $32M

Figure 5.13 Decision Tree Example

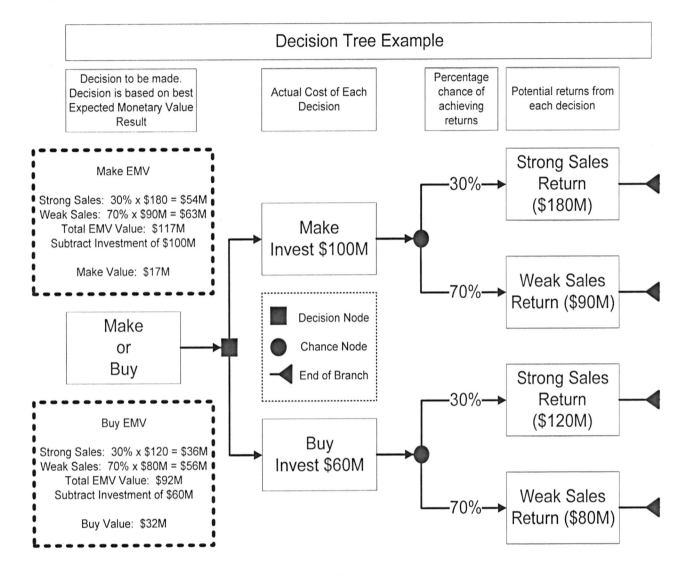

- **Bowtie Analysis:** The Bowtie Analysis method is a risk evaluation method that can be used to analyze and demonstrate causal relationships in high risk scenarios. The method takes its name from the shape of the diagram that you create, which looks like a men's bowtie. A Bowtie diagram does two things. First of all, a Bowtie gives a visual summary of all potential risk scenarios that could exist. Second, the analysis shows measures that can be taken to control a risk scenario. Figure 5.14 shares a simple visual.

Figure 5.14 Bowtie Analysis Example

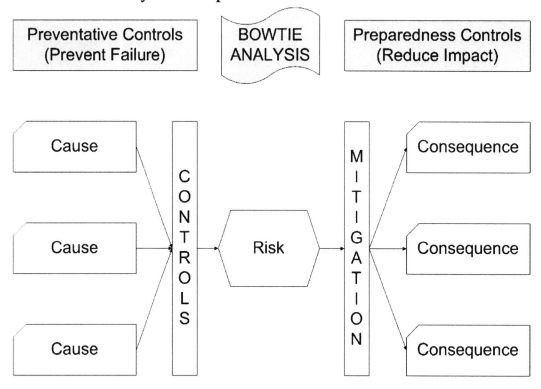

- **Risk Based Critical Chain Analysis:** Risk Based Critical Chain analysis is defined as the use of buffers to mitigate potential high risk network diagram configurations. The example in Figure 5.15 below shows two high risk work packages (B and C). The Project Manager added a 2-day buffer based on risk factors. **Note:** A buffer is considered as non-work time. However, a buffer does extend a schedule.

Figure 5.15 Critical Chain Analysis Illustration

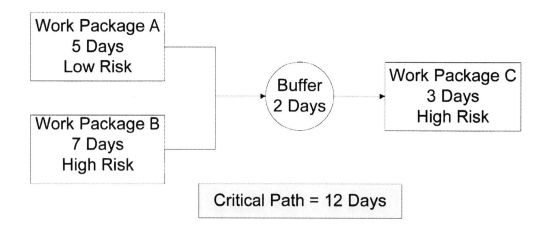

- **Regression Analysis:** In statistical modeling, *regression analysis is a statistical process for estimating the relationships among variables.* It includes many techniques for modeling and analyzing several variables, when the focus is on the relationship between a dependent variable and one or more independent variables (or predictors).[9] Analysis of multiple variables, and their impact on each other, is referred to as Multi-Factor Regression Analysis.

- **System Dynamics (SD):** System dynamics is a methodology and *mathematical modeling technique to frame, understand, and discuss complex issues and problems.* Originally developed in the 1950s to help corporate managers improve their understanding of industrial processes, SD is currently being used throughout the public and private sector for policy analysis and design.[10] It is also used to determine risk factors impacting complex issues and problems confronting a project.

- **Force Field Analysis:** *Force Field Analysis defines accelerators that can move a project toward a successful conclusion and resistors that can move a project toward an unsuccessful conclusion.* Let's put this in the context of risk management. Accelerators correlate well to opportunities. Resistors correlate well with threats. Figure 5.16 provides an visual of Force Field Analysis.

Figure 5.16 Force Field Analysis

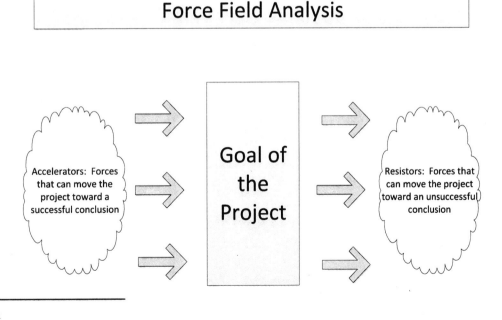

---

[9] Wikipedia
[10] Wikipedia

- **Futures Thinking:** Futures thinking analyzes scenarios *by opening perspectives beyond immediate constraints.* Futures Thinking enhances the capacity of policy-makers and practitioners to anticipate change, grasp opportunities, and cope with threats.

- **Visualization:** Visualization or is *any technique for creating images, diagrams, or animations to communicate a message.* Visualization through visual imagery has been an effective way to communicate both abstract and concrete ideas since the dawn of man.[11] Many team members are visual. By seeing versus simply listening or reading, team members may be able to visualize threats and/or opportunities that would otherwise have been missed.

- **Scenario Planning:** *Scenario planning looks at potential scenarios that may impact a project and determines risk factors for each scenario.* For example, a firm may be looking to change a key customer process. Scenario A may determine risks if the new process is adopted. Scenario B may look at risks if resistance is encountered.

- **Analytical Hierarchy Process (AHP):** AHP is a structured technique for organizing and analyzing complex decisions, based on mathematics and psychology. AHP *provides a comprehensive, hierarchical and rational framework for structuring a decision problem,* for representing and quantifying its elements, for relating those elements to overall goals, and for evaluating alternative solutions. See Figure 5.17 for an illustration of the process.

---

[11] Wikipedia

Figure 5.17 Analytical Hierarchy Process

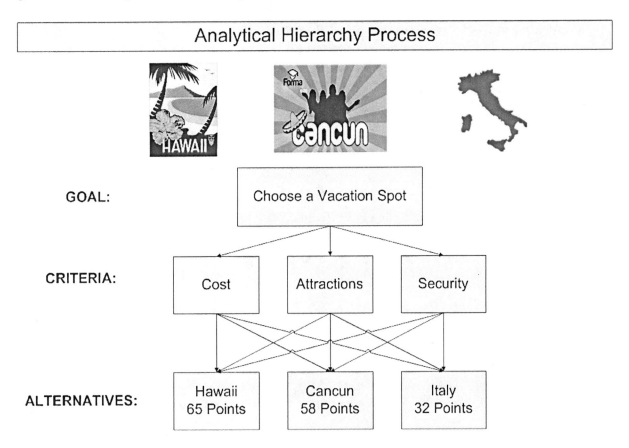

In this example: The goal is to select the most suitable vacation spot from three locations. The factors to be considered are cost, attractions, and security. According to the judgments of the decision makers, Hawaii is the best location, followed by Cancun, then Italy. We can assume there was some type of mathematical determinants that led to Hawaii gaining 65 points.

Perform Quantitative Risk Analysis Output: Update the Risk Register

The Risk Register, and any other applicable project documentation, is updated once again at the end of this step. The Quantitative Risk Analysis process defines the probabilities of meeting defined cost and/or schedule outcomes. Update probability and impact of the risks that most influence project goals either positively or negatively.

Potential Risk Register updates may include, but are not limited to:

- Probabilistic analysis of a project: What are potential time and cost outcomes based on mathematical criteria and analysis?

- Probability of achieving cost and time objectives: Quantitative Risk Analysis allows factoring risk of into budget and schedule estimates. Adjusted data can be compared against original cost and time estimates.

- Prioritized list of quantified risks: What risks are most likely to occur based on new numeric analysis results?

- Trends in quantified risk analysis: A trend of mathematical outcomes may be necessitated to determine if the impact of risk is decreasing or increasing as the project progresses.

- The Risk Register is updated based on the results of the Perform Quantitative Risk Analysis process, as shown in the figure below. Note that the Perform Quantitative Risk Analysis process is Step 4 in the Risk Management Process.

Figure 5.18 Risk Register Update

Risk	Cause	Risk Owner	Category	Risk Response	Probability Risk Rating	Impact Risk Rating	Risk Score
		Initial		Initial	Update in Step 4	Update in Step 4	Update in Step 4
					Update in Step 4	Update in Step 4	Update in Step 4

The Risk Register is updated at the conclusion of the Perform Quantitative Risk Analysis process.

Perform Qualitative Risk Analysis: Keys to Success

- *Perform Qualitative Risk Analysis*: Complete the Perform Qualitative Risk Analysis process *before* accomplishing the Perform Quantitative Risk Analysis process. Ensure the highest priority risks are evaluated during this process for their impact on the project. The Perform Qualitative Risk Analysis process provides initial risk prioritization.

- *Modeling*: The Quantitative Risk Analysis process uses models. Select the right model that supports project analysis needs such as project schedules, individual cost estimates, decision trees, etc.

- *Quality Data*: The Quantitative Risk Analysis process is objective. Ensure data sources are accurate and unbiased. Use tools and techniques such as Interviews that help attain expert input.

- *Bias*: It is important to reduce cognitive and motivational bias as defined earlier. Try to find unbiased sources to help score risks as accurately as possible.

- *Relationships*: Look for relationships between multiple risks. Know how one risk may impact or lead to others.

- *Stakeholder Tolerance*: Measure stakeholder tolerance levels for risk and incorporate these into your final scoring. If your Sponsor tells you budget is not an issue, giving cost risks a high impact score is not realistic. Spend your time managing the risks that matter!

- *Repeating*: It is a best practice to re-accomplish Quantitative Risk Analysis at the completion of the Plan Risk Responses process. This iterative practice is part of the Control Risks process.

- *Quantitative Risk Analysis:* The best evaluation of risk includes a combination of Qualitative and Quantitative methods. This may not always be feasible. Quantitative Risk Analysis is our next subject.

Qualitative Versus Quantitative Risk Analysis

The Perform Qualitative Risk Analysis process is always performed, but the Perform Quantitative Risk Analysis process is situational. The table below shares key distinctions between the two risk analysis processes. These distinctions must be understood for testing purposes.

Figure 5.19 Qualitative Risk Analysis Versus Quantitative Risk Analysis

Perform Qualitative Risk Analysis Process	Perform Quantitative Risk Analysis Process
Subjective	Objective
Always accomplished	Accomplished when there is value to expend time and effort
Fast	Takes time and expertise
Addresses individual risks	Predicts likely outcomes based on review of multiple risks
Scores risks using probability × impact	Uses numerical analysis such as Probability Distribution, EMV, Decision Trees, etc.
Prioritizes individual risks	Identifies risks with greatest impact to project objectives
Output is a prioritized list of risks	Output is a probability of meeting defined project outcomes
Risk Register is updated at the conclusion of both activities	

Activity 5: Perform Quantitative Risk Analysis

Directions: Complete the activities below. Answers are in Appendix A.

Part I: Three Point Estimating

Three estimates are given. Calculate the best estimate using Three Point Averaging and Three Point PERT. Then calculate the Standard Deviation.

Estimate to Complete Activity	Number of Days Estimated
Pessimistic	28 Days
Most Likely	12 Days
Optimistic	8 Days

Three Point Averaging	
PERT	
Standard Deviation	

Part II: EMV

Five risks impacting your project are identified as follows. How much in total Contingency Reserves should be requested?

RISK	PROBABILITY	IMPACT	EMV
A	10%	($20,000)	
B	40%	$30,000	
C	30%	$27,000	
D	50%	$18,000	
E	25%	$44,000	
TOTAL			

Risk D occurs. How much remains in the Contingency Reserves?

Part III: Monte Carlo Analysis

What is the probability of achieving a goal of spending $40M?

The organization wants to have an 80% probability of achieving cost objectives. What is the cost to achieve 80%?

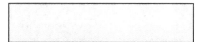

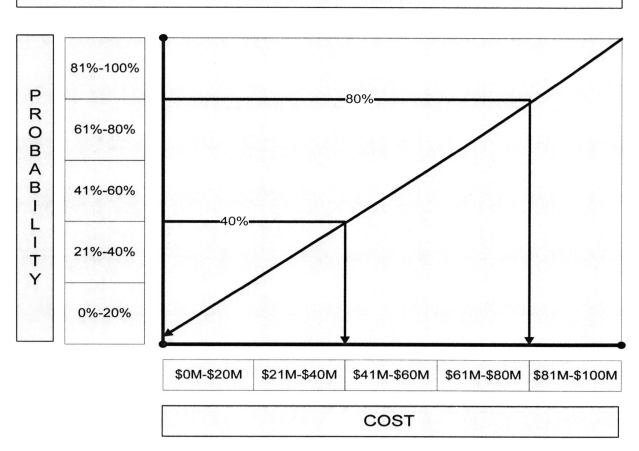

Part IV: Decision Tree

What is the EMV of the Make decision?

What is the EMV of the Buy decision?

What is the best decision based on EMV?

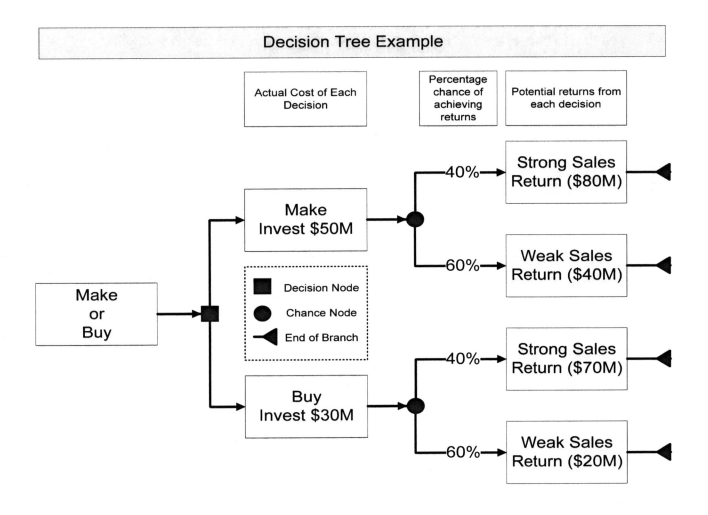

Decision Tree Example

Actual Cost of Each Decision	Percentage chance of achieving returns	Potential returns from each decision

Make Invest $50M

40% → Strong Sales Return ($80M)

60% → Weak Sales Return ($40M)

Make or Buy

- ■ Decision Node
- ● Chance Node
- ◀ End of Branch

Buy Invest $30M

40% → Strong Sales Return ($70M)

60% → Weak Sales Return ($20M)

Part V: Tools and Techniques Match Game

Match the tool and technique definition to the correct response. Answers are in Appendix A.

Perform Quantitative Risk Analysis Tool and Technique Search Activity	Response
1. Any technique for creating images, diagrams, or animations to communicate a message.	
2. Analysis method that uses several What If scenarios to calculate potential results. Modeling technique that helps determine which risks have the greatest impact on a project.	
3. Method used widely to establish Contingency Reserve requirements for both budget and schedule. Quantified by multiplying probability times the best or worst case cost/time scenario.	
4. Simulation technique that furnishes the decision-maker with a range of possible outcomes and the probabilities they will occur for any choice of action.	
5. A bar graph that shows the best case and worst case cost or benefit scenario for a risk.	
6. Defines accelerators that can move a project toward a successful conclusion, and resistors that can move a project toward an unsuccessful conclusion.	
7. Technique includes a mix of open-ended and prepared questions. Begin with open-ended questions to gain insight from the interviewer. Follow up with prepared questions.	
8. Looks at potential scenarios that may impact a project and determines risk factors for each scenario.	
9. Provides a comprehensive, hierarchical and rational framework for structuring a decision problem, for representing and quantifying its elements, for relating those elements to overall goals, and for evaluating alternative solutions.	
10. Estimates the potential of a risk event to occur over a pre-described range, generally over a normal distribution.	
11. Analyzes scenarios by opening perspectives beyond immediate constraints. Enhances the capacity of policy-makers and practitioners to anticipate change, grasp opportunities, and cope with threats.	
12. Describes a scenario under consideration and uses available data to determine the most economic approach. The primary objective is selecting the scenario that provides the best overall Expected Monetary Value (EMV).	

Activity V: Choose from the following:

A. Interviewing

B. Probability Distribution

C. Sensitivity Analysis

D. Tornado Diagram

E. Analytical Hierarchy Process

F. Monte Carlo Technique

G. Expected Monetary Value (EMV)

H. Decision Tree Analysis

I. Scenario Planning

J. Visualization

K. Futures Thinking

L. Force Field Analysis

Chapter 6: Plan Risk Responses

Process 5: Plan Risk Responses

Plan Risk Responses is the fifth process in Project Risk Management. The primary objectives are to validate risk responses and Risk Owners identified during the Identify Risks process, or develop risk responses for risks on the Urgent List and assign Risk Owners if not previously accomplished.

Seven distinct responses can be taken to address risk. Three responses are reserved for negative risks. Three responses are reserved for positive risks. One response is used for both negative and positive risks. An in-depth review of each response will be discussed in the tools and techniques section.

- Risk Owners are confirmed or assigned during the Plan Risk Responses process. Risk Owners develop responses, monitor risk status, and implement Contingency Plans and Fallback Plans, if required. Risk Owners can be any stakeholder in the project. They are *best* used during the processes of Plan Risk Responses and Control Risks.

- You may encounter a definition of a Risk Action Owner. This individual is assigned by a Risk Owner to help implement approved risk responses.

- The primary response to a risk is referred to as either a Contingency Plan or a Risk Response Plan. You may wish to develop a secondary plan should the Contingency Plan fail called a Fallback Plan. There may be times when Contingency Plans or Fallback Plans cannot be developed. The risk must be accepted when this is the case.

- Document Secondary Risks in the Risk Register as well. A Secondary Risk is one that results from a risk response. For example, a response to use a vendor to perform project work could lead to potential vendor management risks. Document the vendor management risks as Secondary Risks. A Secondary Risk should *never* have a higher Risk Rating than the primary risk associated with it.

- Residual Risks must be accounted for as well. A Residual Risk is one that remains after a Risk Response Plan or Contingency Plan is implemented. For example, a response may address 80% of the risk impact. The remaining 20% represents the Residual Risk. Contingency Plans or Fallback Plans should be in place to respond to known Residual Risks. New Residual Risks may be discovered during a Risk Audit.

If so, log the Residual Risk on the Risk Register and begin the Perform Qualitative Risk Analysis process.

The Plan Risk Response process can lead to a Go/No Go decision. A No Go decision could occur if there are critical risks for which no responses can be developed. A No Go decision could also result if the Project Risk Score was well above acceptable thresholds and there was little you could do to address the situation.

- *The level of detail defined in a risk response should be based on the priority of the risk.* A high priority risk would warrant greater levels of detail than a lower priority risk.

- Risk responses may lead to additional work that could cause the Schedule Baseline and/or Cost Performance Baseline to change. Solicit approval for this type of risk response from the Project Sponsor.

An overview of the end to end Plan Risk Response Process is shown in Figure 6.1:

Figure 6.1 Plan Risk Responses Process

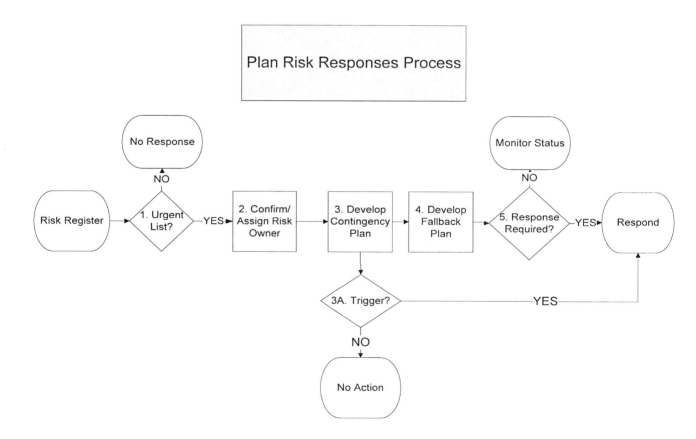

1. All risks should be identified in the Risk Register. Generally, responses are developed for those risks listed on the Urgent List.

2. Risk Owners are identified initially during the Identify Risks process. They are confirmed during the Plan Risk Responses process.

3. Risk Owners develop Contingency Plans or Risk Response Plans. They also identify potential Triggers. Triggers are any event that provide an early warning that a risk is about to occur. The response plan is implemented when a Trigger occurs.

4. Fallback Plans are also developed by the Risk Owner. These plans are implemented if the Contingency Plan does not provide the desired response.

5. Risk Owners monitor all risks they are assigned as owners. They provide periodic status updates as required. They respond to risks when required. They team with Risk Action Owners when responding.

Plan Risk Responses Process

The Plan Risk Responses process consists of inputs, tools and techniques, and outputs shown in Figure 6.2 below.

Figure 6.2 Plan Risk Responses Process

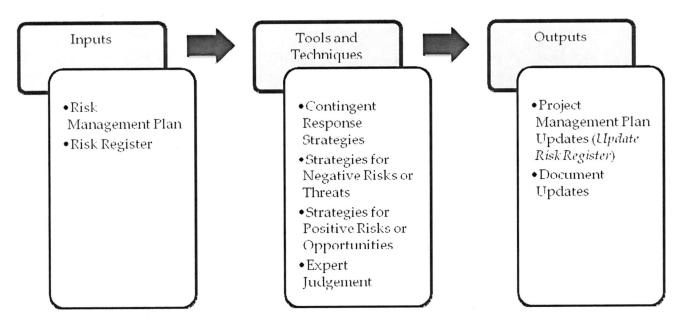

Plan Risk Responses: Inputs

Only two inputs are required to complete the Plan Risk Responses process. Both are outputs of previous overall Risk Management processes.

Input	Applicability
Risk Management Plan	Defines roles and responsibilities and methodologies to evaluate risks.
Risk Register	Provides the initial list of risks to be evaluated. The Risk Register will be updated during this process.

Plan Risk Responses: Tools and Techniques

Tools and techniques are used to develop risk responses. Here is a list of applicable tools and techniques supporting this process.

- **Contingent Response Strategies**: There are times when events happen that indicate a risk will soon occur. These events are called predefined conditions, or *Triggers*. When Triggers occur, initiate your Risk Response Plan. For example, the project defines a contingency response strategy to order 10,000 spare parts from Vendor B if Vendor A misses planned shipments of spare parts by more than two days. The Trigger occurs when Vendor A misses the shipment by more than two days.

- **Strategies for Negative Risks and Threats**: There are four strategies for dealing with negative risks. They include:

  - *Avoid (Avoidance):* The focus of this strategy is to eliminate the cause of the risk. Try to take action to ensure the risk does not occur. This is often accomplished by removing people and/or activities.

  - *Transfer (Transference)*: This response transfers accountability and responsibility of a risk to a third party. The third party actually performs the work or takes accountability. A cost is usually incurred when using the transfer or transference response. A prime example of transference is the purchase of insurance.

  - *Mitigate (Mitigation):* This response takes actions to reduce the probability of the risk occurring or the impact of risk if it occurs. This could be thought of as developing a Plan B. An example is training. We try to reduce the probability and impact of employees performing poorly on the job by training them.

o *Accept (Acceptance):* This response entails taking no immediate action until the risk occurs. Two types of acceptance strategies are described below. One is *passive,* and the other is *active.*

- Acceptance is a response strategy appropriate for *both* negative and positive risks.

- A Contingency Plan or Fallback Plan may be developed for a risk you plan to accept. However, the response will not be initiated until the risk occurs.

- Acceptance is often the only choice when risks are generated from external sources, or when risk responses are beyond the control of the Project Manager.

- *Passive Acceptance*: This type of acceptance occurs when no Contingency Plans are created to address the risk.

- *Active Acceptance*: Develop Contingency Plans to address the risk when it occurs. Active Acceptance is a solid option when necessary to convince risk-averse stakeholders that a response plan for accepted risks is in place.

- **Strategies for Positive Risks or Opportunities:** Four strategies deal with positive risks. They include:

o *Exploit (Exploitation):* This is a response that takes action to make a cause occur. Steps are taken to ensure the risk happens. It may require additional time or resources to use the exploit response method. *This is the opposite of the Avoid response.*

o *Share (Sharing):* This response enlists the support of a third party to take advantage of the opportunities presented by a positive risk event. Partnering with a third party allows both parties to share in the benefits. *This is the opposite of the Transfer response.*

- *Teaming Agreements* are an example of a Share response. These agreements are quite common between established sellers and buyers with a long-term relationship. Teaming can occur between external and internal stakeholders.

- o *Enhance (Enhancing):* This response aims to increase the probability of the risk occurring or the impact of a risk if it occurs. Incentives are a common example of an enhance response. *This is the opposite of the Mitigate response.*

  - *Crashing* is a common form of Enhancement or Mitigation. However, Crashing can increase costs of the project.

- o *Accept (Acceptance):* Acceptance is a feasible risk response for both negative and positive risks.

Figure 6.3 is a visual provided to aid in understanding specific risk response types and when they are potentially applied. Plan Risk Responses is Step 5 in the Risk Management Process, as defined in the *PMBOK,* Chapter 11.

Figure 6.3 Risk Response Strategies

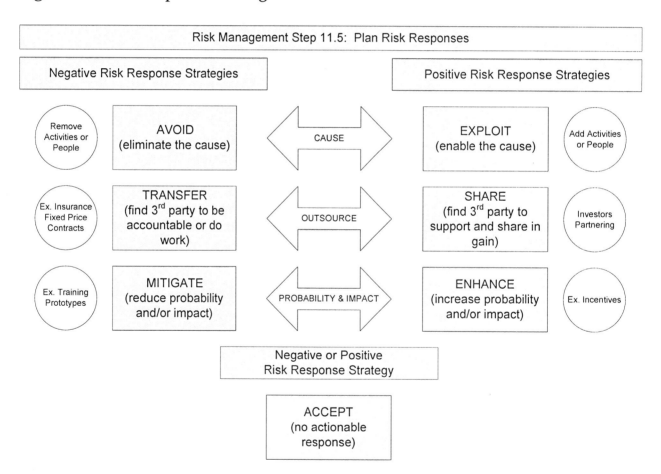

Plan Risk Responses: Outputs

Two outputs are in the Plan Risk Responses process.

- **Project Management Plan Updates:** Update the Risk Register and/or the Risk Management Plan as required at the conclusion of the Plan Risk Responses process. A number of other key project management planning documents are also updated as a result of Risk Management Process activities. Residual Risks and Secondary Risks are also documented.

- **Project Document Updates:** Risk integrates with many other areas. Updating project documents is a potential result of the Plan Risk Responses process.

Figure 6.4 below shows specific areas in the Risk Register updated after Process 5 of the Risk Management Process.

Figure 6.4 Risk Register Update

Risk	Cause	Risk Owner	Category	Risk Response	Probability Risk Rating	Impact Risk Rating	Risk Score
		Update in Process 5		Update Process 5	Update Process 5	Update Process 5	Update Process 5
		Update in Process 5		Update Process 5	Update Process 5	Update Process 5	Update Process 5

Risk Owners and risk responses may be updated at the conclusion of the Plan Risk Responses process. Risk Ratings and Risk Scores may be updated based on responses developed as well.

Plan Risk Responses: Keys to Success

- *People*: Ensure risk responses are communicated with impacted stakeholders. Ensure all key stakeholders understand their specific roles and responsibilities. Do not assume!

- *Planning*: Base the detail of risk responses on the priority of the risk. Ensure key criteria as timing, resource needs, budget impacts, and schedule implications are addressed. Remember that the Risk Owner should develop, manage, and implement risk responses. Risk Action Owners assist Risk Owners during responses.

- *Consistency*: Ensure responses are consistent with organizational values, project objectives, and stakeholder expectations. Ensure responses are technically feasible and can be accomplished as planned.

- *Analysis*: Ensure the link between the risk and the risk response is clear. Solicit agreement and buy-in for all responses from applicable stakeholders.

- *Opportunities and Threats*: Remember, there are two classifications of risk. Develop responses for both positive and negative risks.

- *Documentation Updates*: Ensure that agreed upon responses are integrated into the Project Management Plan. Ensure technical documentation is updated as new information becomes available through risk responses.

- *Project Manager Support*: The Risk Owner is responsible to implement Contingency Plans. The Project Manager should respect this role and not get involved unless absolutely necessary. The Project Manager should adjust the severity of the Risk Response Plan, if necessary, during implementation.

Activity 6: Plan Risk Responses

Read the scenarios. Which risk strategy should be used in each scenario? Choose Avoid, Transfer, Mitigate, Accept, Exploit, Share, or Enhance. Answers are found in Appendix A.

Scenario	Response Being Used
1. You determine a planned feature is not technically feasible. You eliminate the feature from the Project Scope.	
2. You can get a 10% discount from a key supplier if you order 100,000 units. Your project requires 80,000 units. You contact other Project Managers to determine if there are needs for the additional units to gain the discount.	
3. There is an opportunity to save over $10,000 if you accept a seller's offer. Your team agrees the offer is good but determines not to pursue it at this time.	
4. You learn of an opportunity to cut three weeks off your project schedule. Resources are available that allow you to crash key critical activities to increase the probability of achieving the time savings.	
5. You learn that a competitor is attempting to replicate one of your key products. You add additional technical features that cannot be duplicated that will prevent the competitor from building a like product.	
6. You add incentives to increase the probability of early completion of a key work package by a critical vendor.	
7. Your team does not have the expertise to eliminate a key safety risk. You spend $10,000 to enlist the support of a third-party vendor who will respond to the risk.	
8. You learn that a new external regulation was discovered that adds risk to completing your project within budget. You determine that you will deal with any risks that materialize when they occur.	
9. A new Project Manager heard there is a risk response that can be used to address both positive and negative risks.	
10. There are two key risks to your project schedule. You develop a training program to respond to the first. For the second risk, you develop a prototype that will enhance testing.	
11. You develop some Teaming Agreements with a key supplier to improve levels of cooperation and improve Return on Investment.	
12. You are told there are four potential responses to address negative risks or threats. You remember Accept, Transfer, and Avoid. Which did you miss?	
13. You add an additional vendor at a cost of $25,000 with the expertise to ensure an identified risk event occurs that will lead to opportunities to reduce time spent on critical path activities.	

Chapter 7: Control Risks

Process 6: Control Risks

Control Risks is the sixth and final process in Project Risk Management. This process is the "C" in the PIER-C methodology.

Risk is an iterative process. Risk factors come and go and conditions continually change. Note that risk is not a one-time activity! The ultimate goal of Control Risks is to stay current on project risk. Control Risks is the process of:

- Ensuring the effectiveness of the Project Risk Management Process

- Tracking identified risks

- Monitoring Residual Risks and Secondary Risks

- Identifying, analyzing, and planning for new risks

- Keeping track of risks listed on the Risk Register Watch List

- Reanalyzing existing risks as conditions change

- Monitoring risk Trigger conditions

- Implementing Risk Response Plans, as needed

- Evaluating effectiveness of risk responses

- Updating the Risk Register as required

- Submitting formal changes when necessary to update Contingency Plans

A Project Manager may be called upon to respond to a previously unidentified or unknown risk. This response is defined as a *workaround*.

It should be noted that this is the only process in Project Risk Management that is not part of the Planning Process Group. *Control Risks falls under the Monitoring and Controlling Process Group*.

Control Risks Process

The Control Risks process consists of inputs, tools and techniques, and outputs shown in Figure 7.1 below.

Figure 7.1 Control Risks Process

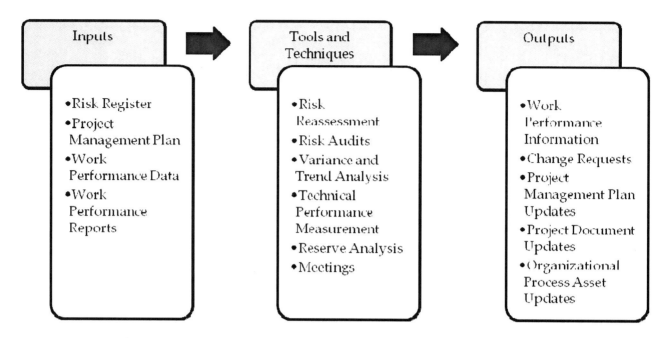

Control Risks: Inputs

Four inputs are required to conduct the Control Risks process.

Input	Applicability
Risk Register	Provides the initial list of risks to be evaluated. The Risk Register will be added to and updated during this process.
Project Management Plan	This is the approved plan that contains the Risk Management Plan that describes methodology, roles, reserve considerations, etc.
Work Performance Data	Raw data generated from all Project Executing Process Group processes. Work Performance Data is reviewed, analyzed, and transformed into more useable Work Performance Information.
Work Performance Reports	These reports include Earned Value Technique data, such as schedule and cost status. They also include forecasting data, which is critical to recognition and control of risks.

Work Performance Reports: It will benefit you to understand how Work Performance Reports used in the Control Risks process are generated.

- *Work Performance Data (WPD)* is an input to all processes in the Monitor and Control Process Group. WPD is generated in all processes supporting the Executing Process Group. As stated previously, WPD is raw data generated from multiple stakeholders. During the Control Risks process, WPD potentially impacting project risks are reviewed and analyzed to determine potential impact.

- *Work Performance Information (WPI)* is an output of all Monitor and Control processes. As you will see, WPI is an output of the Control Risks process. WPI collects pertinent WPD, and converts it into more useable information that can be used to feed the overall project Work Performance Report.

- *Work Performance Reports (WPR)* consolidate all WPI generated from multiple Monitor and Control processes and puts this information into a comprehensive project status report that covers all aspects of the project. WPR are a key input for the Control Risks process. In essence, the overall status of a project can let a Project Manager better determine if risk is impacting results.

Figure 7.2 below shows the relationship among WPD, WPI, and WPR.

Figure 7.2 Work Performance Report Generation Process

Control Risks: Tools and Techniques

Key tools and techniques are used to monitor and control risks.

- **Risk Reassessment**: Risk monitoring and control often identifies new risks and requires reassessment of existing risks. In addition, risks that are outdated should be closed. Risk Reassessment also ensures new risks are identified when changes to the project are made.

  o A *Risk Review* is used to analyze potential risk responses to see if they are still appropriate. This is a part of Risk Reassessment. A Risk Review may include changing the order or priority of risks, adjusting the severity of existing risks, or monitoring Residual Risks.

- Many events can drive the need for Risk Reassessment. These events include occurrences of unknown risks, evaluation of change requests, project re-planning, or conducting a phase end review. Requirements for Risk Reassessment should be included in the Risk Management Plan.

- **Risk Audits:** Risk Audits examine responses to risk and answer the question, "How did we do?" Risk Audits also measure the overall effectiveness of the Risk Management Process. Periodic Risk Audits should be performed to evaluate the strengths and weaknesses of the overall Risk Management Process. Risk Audit requirements are also identified in the Risk Management Plan. *Most Residual Risks are identified during Risk Audits.*

- **Variance and Trend Analysis:** Trends should be observed and deviations noted. This tool and technique compares planned results with actual results. PMI contends that Earned Value Technique is an effective method to perform this analysis.

- **Technical Performance Measurement:** The Quality Management Plan defines targets, metrics, etc. Technical performance measurement determines if the actual technical performance achieved matches planned technical performance specifications.

- **Reserve Analysis:** Management Reserves or Contingency Reserves for risk may or may not be granted. If provided, the Project Manager must manage the reserves and ensure they are allocated *only* in the event of risk occurrence. Some people will look upon this reserve as a great source for extras. Remember that Management Reserves are designated for *unknown unknowns* (Unknown Risks), while Contingency Reserves are designated for *known unknowns* (Known Risks).

- **Meetings:** Some portion of status meetings, or a separate meeting, is essential to address risks. Risks should be treated with importance, rather than as a "by the way" subject. *PMI recommends a weekly meeting to discuss risk.* Periodic meetings will allow stakeholders to identify newly discovered risks throughout the life of the project.

Control Risks: Outputs

The key outputs of the Control Risks process include updates and change requests. A review of each output in more detail follows:

- **Risk Register Updates:** The outcomes of Risk Reassessment and Risk Audits may lead to updates. Actual outcomes from responses may require changes to the Risk Register.

- **Organizational Process Asset Updates:** Lessons Learned may lead to updated Risk Breakdown Structures (RBSs). Other project management templates may require updates as well.

- **Change Requests:** Corrective or preventative change requests may be required to change Contingency Plans or Fallback Plans.

    o Change requests may also be required to bring a project into compliance with the Project Management Plan. This is especially true when *Gold Platers* cause *Scope Creep.* We discuss these two definitions further during our discussion of Project Scope Management in Chapter 9 of this book.

- **Project Management Plan and Document Updates:** The Risk Management Plan, Risk Register, and other key project management planning documents may require updates. These are all living documents.

Control Risks: Keys to Success

- *Integration*: Ensure the Control Risks process is included as part of the approved and accepted Project Management Plan. The Risk Management Plan should define key Control Risks activities.

- *Communication*: Maintain open and honest communications with Risk Owners and Risk Action Owners.

    o Include all key stakeholders when communicating risk status information. The project Risk Register should be available anytime to all stakeholders.

    o Watch for Triggers that signal the onset of risks. Add new Triggers for risks as they are identified. Develop Contingent Response Strategies.

- *Awareness*: Ensure current risk status is included as an agenda item in project status meetings. Ensure that the value of risk management activities is evangelized in a manner that helps maintain stakeholder commitment to the process.

- *Reserve Management*: Track Contingency Reserves and Management Reserves. Ensure there are adequate reserves remaining and are used for their designated purpose. Request additional Contingency Reserves when needed. Return Contingency Reserves no longer required when risks are closed.

- *Updates:* Ensure all changes are reflected in the Risk Register. Add new risks, reprioritize existing risks, and eliminate risks no longer applicable.

- *Lessons Learned*: Take the time to record what is learned for the use of future Project Managers. Record both positive and negative risk related lessons. PMI recommends that Lessons Learned sessions be conducted when completing key project phases or meeting essential project milestones. History does repeat itself! Lessons Learned help ensure positive history is repeated and negative history is prevented.

Activity 7: Control Risks Concepts

Directions: Key definitions and concepts are discussed in the Control Risks process. Match the definition to the responses provided. Answers are found in Appendix A.

Control Risks Definition and Concept Activity	Response
1. Provides reserves to support risk identified on the Risk Register.	
2. Examines and documents the effectiveness of risk responses and the overall Risk Management Process.	
3. Risks that may result directly from implementing a planned Contingency Plan.	
4. Provides funds to support Emergent Risks.	
5. May be required to request additional reserves for a newly identified risk response.	
6. Part of a Risk Reassessment that may include changing the order or priority of risks, adjusting the severity of existing risks, or monitoring Residual Risks.	
7. Risks that remain after implementing a planned Risk Response Plan. They must be accounted for on the Risk Register.	
8. Compares project technical accomplishments to the schedule defining when technical achievement is required.	
9. A process that identifies new risks, reassesses current risks, and closes out risks that are no longer applicable.	
10. An output of the Control Risks process that uses Work Performance Data to compile.	

Activity 7: Choose from the following:

A. Risk Review

B. Risk Audit

C. Risk Reassessment

D. Residual Risks

E. Secondary Risks

F. Change Requests

G. Management Reserves

H. Contingency Reserves

I. Technical Performance Measurement

J. Work Performance Information

Chapter 8: Risk Governance

Risk Governance was a specific area in the PMI-RMP Body of Knowledge. Though no longer a stand-alone domain, Risk Governance is a key area of knowledge you should know for the PMI-RMP test.

General Risk Governance Concepts

Risk Governance is the process of ensuring risk policies and procedures are understood, followed, consistently applied, and effective. Risk Governance may be implemented by the Project Manager, a PMO, or even a specific organizational Risk Governance body. Actual ownership is based on the priority, size, and importance of the project.

Risk Governance includes any tools, techniques, and outputs from the Control Risks process.

- Risk Governance looks at the complex web of actors, rules, policy, procedures, and methods regarding risk information collection, communication, analysis, and how decisions are made.

- Risk Governance keys on consistent risk assessment, risk management, and risk communication.

- Risk Governance ensures the goals and objectives of the Board of Directors and company stockholders are met.

Risk Governance may include *creation of standard policies and procedures* to ensure risk compliance. These policies may impact areas such as:

- Required levels of sponsorship based on key considerations, such as cost of projects, priorities, etc.

- Standard templates, Resource Breakdown Structures, Organizational Process Assets, or risk processes.

- Organizational risk tolerance standards and/or risk category thresholds.

- Standardized quality management planning to include metric, target, and Process Improvement Plan development.

- Creation of metrics to guide organizational risk management activities.

- Standardized risk management planning to include Risk Breakdown Structures (RBSs) and methods to identify risks. Standardized processing of Lessons Learned. Data collection and standard Corporate Knowledge Base direction.

- Standardized policies and procedures regarding Risk Reassessments, Risk Reviews, and Risk Audits.

- Policies and procedures to conduct and share Lessons Learned. Lessons Learned should include what went well, what can go better, and what can be done differently in the future.

Two organizations impact Risk Governance.

- Risk Governance may follow principles defined by the *International Risk Governance Council (IRGC).* This organization's primary goal is to facilitate understanding and manage risks that impact society, human health, safety, and the environment as a whole.

- PMI strives to be compatible with approaches defined by the *International Organization for Standardization, or ISO.* ISO develops standards based on best practices and encourages their use by all who subscribe to ISO methodology. ISO guides the PMI basic approach to quality management to include standardized tools as Six Sigma, Total Quality Management (TQM), and FMEA.

Risk Governance ensures risk management efforts are focused to meet organizational needs. It ensures there is a cultural norm that supports risk management activities.

Other Governance Areas

Earned Value Technique

A key consideration of Risk Governance is performance reporting. Earned Value Technique is PMI's preferred method of performance reporting.

A few key terms must be understood to calculate Earned Value Technique.

- Earned Value (EV) is the value of work performed. A typical calculation may look like this: 65% of a $100,000 project is complete. Multiply .65 × $100,000 to determine the EV. EV = $65,000.

- Planned Value (PV) is the amount of budget planned to be used at a given point in the project. It is determined that the project should be 70% complete to this point. Multiply .7 × $100,000 to determine the PV. PV = $70,000.

- Actual Costs (AC) are the actual cost of the project to date. For example, actual costs for the sample project referenced above are $75,000.

- Budget at Completion (BAC) is an expression of the total budget for the project. Assume BAC is $100,000 for this project scenario.

The Earned Value Technique values described above are used to perform Earned Value Technique calculations. A review of our values follows:

A. EV = $65,000

B. PV = $70,000

C. AC = $75,000

D. BAC = $100,000

The illustration in Figure 8.1 uses these values to perform Earned Value Technique calculations:

Figure 8.1 Earned Value Technique Illustration

Earned Value Technique Calculation	Formula
1. Schedule Variance (SV)	Earned Value (EV) – Planned Value (PV) $65,000 - $70,000 = -$5,000
2. Cost Variance (CV)	Earned Value (EV) – Actual Costs (AC) $65,000 - $75,000 = -$10,000
3. Schedule Performance Index (SPI)	EV/PV $65,000/$70,000 = .93
4. Cost Performance Index (CPI)	EV/AC $65,000/$75,000 = .87
5. Estimate to Completion (ETC)	Budget at Completion (BAC)/CPI $100,000/.87 = $114,943

Earned Value Technique Notes:

1. **Schedule Variance:** A SV of 0 is an indicator that the project is on schedule. Negative SV is an indicator that the project is behind schedule. The example above of -$5,000 fits this definition. Positive SV is an indicator that the project is ahead of schedule.

2. **Cost Variance:** A CV of 0 is an indicator that the project is on budget. Negative CV is an indicator that the project is behind budget. The example above of -$10,000 fits this definition. Positive CV is an indicator that the project is ahead of budget.

3. **Schedule Performance Index:** A SPI of 1.0 is an indicator that the project is on schedule. An SPI less than 1.0 is an indicator that the project is behind schedule. The example above of .93 fits this definition. A SPI greater than 1.0 is an indicator that the project is ahead of schedule.

4. **Cost Performance Index:** A CPI of 1.0 is an indicator that the project is on budget. A CPI less than 1.0 is an indicator that the project is behind budget. The example above of .87 fits this definition. A CPI greater than 1.0 is an indicator that the project is ahead of budget.

5. **Estimate to Completion:** The project in this scenario is behind on both schedule and budget. The ETC based on the current trend is $114,943. This represents a $14,943 cost overrun unless actions to counteract the situation are taken.

Contract Types

Some organizations dictate certain contract type requirements as part of their Risk Governance policy and procedure. Remember who assumes the *Cost Risk* for the following contracts:

- **Fixed Price:** A Fixed Price Contract is a price provided by a seller to complete a contract. *Cost Risk is on the seller.*

  o A Fixed Price Contract is used when the project service or product is well defined. A seller provides a price proposal to perform the work exactly as described by a potential buyer. A Fixed Price Contract may be adjusted.

- o A Firm Fixed Price (FFP) Contract is a stricter version of a basic Fixed Price Contract. An FFP Contract is not normally changed. The contract price remains unchanged throughout the life of the contract.

- **Cost Reimbursement:** A buyer proposes work and contracts the seller's expertise. Total costs are not known until the end of the contract. *Cost Risk is on the buyer.*

  - o A Cost Reimbursement Contract is generally used when a buyer knows the functionality they need from a product. However, they do not have the expertise to build the project. They are purchasing this expertise.

  - o A Cost Plus Percentage of Cost *poses highest Cost Risk* to a buyer.

- **Time and Material:** This type of contract is similar to Cost Reimbursement. Cost Risk is on the buyer.

  - o Time and Material Contracts are quick, short in duration, and are generally used for services.

Activity 8: Risk Governance

Directions: Read the statements below. Determine if the statements are true or false. Answers are in Appendix A.

Statement	True or False
1. Risk Governance is accomplished primarily during the Plan Risk Management process of Project Risk Management.	
2. ISO is an organization developed to inspect final project deliverables for technical compliance.	
3. A $50,000 project is 50% complete. Actual Costs are $30,000. CPI is .83.	
4. The buyer accepts the Cost Risk for a Cost Reimbursement type of contract.	
5. A Cost Plus Percentage of Cost contract poses the lowest level of risk to a buyer.	
6. Identify Risks is the process of ensuring risk policies and procedures are understood, followed, consistently applied, and effective.	
7. A key Risk Governance activity is the development of metrics to guide organizational risk management activities.	
8. Risk Governance is concerned with how policies and procedures are implemented, rather than the creation of policies and procedures.	
9. The primary goal of the IRGC is to facilitate understanding and manage risks that impact society, human health, safety, and the environment as a whole.	
10. Lessons Learned meetings should be limited to discuss solely what went well and what could go better.	
11. A quick review of your project reveals a CPI of 1.2. You should conclude your project is behind on budget.	

Chapter 9: Other Key Concepts from the *PMBOK*

Introduction to Project Management

There are four key areas to remember from Chapters 1 through 4 of the *PMBOK*. They include:

- Steps in the PMI Framework

- Integrated Change Control Functions

- Types of Organizations

- Understand Project Environments

PMI Framework: Know the five Process Groups in the order they occur, beginning with the Initiating Process Group through the Closing Process Group.

Figure 9.1 PMI Framework

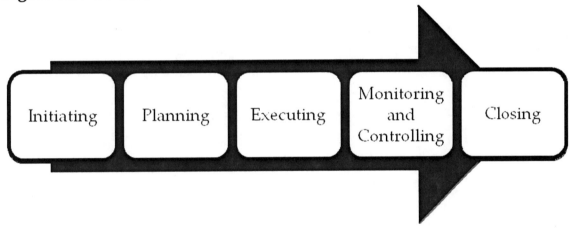

Integrated Change Control Functions: Remember the following facts regarding Integrated Change Control:

- Integrated Change Control procedures must be defined for every project. Procedures for reviewing changes should include identifying any new risks that may be introduced by a recommended change.

- A Change Control Log should be created as well. The Change Control Log lists all change requests processed in support of the project. It also provides status of changes to include those approved and declined. The project Change Control Log should be reviewed as a potential source of risks.

- Communicating approval or denial of recommended changes is a vital activity of Integrated Change Control.

- Configuration Management is part of Integrated Change Control. It focuses on controlling changes to the functional and physical characteristics of the project's product or service.

Types of Organizations: There are three primary organizational models to be aware of as shown in Figure 9.2:

Figure 9.2 Organizational Types

Organizational Structure	Key Attributes
FUNCTIONAL (Most Common Form)	<ul><li>Each employee has one manager</li><li>Staff members are grouped by specialty</li><li>For functional organizations, think Silo</li><li>Team members normally communicate up and down the Silo</li></ul>
PROJECTIZED	<ul><li>Team members are co-located</li><li>Organization focus is projects</li><li>Project Managers have high levels of authority and independence</li><li>Personnel are assigned and report to a Project Manager</li></ul>
MATRIX (The Default for PMI Questions)	<ul><li>A blend of Functional and Projectized organizations</li><li>Resources are borrowed from other functions</li><li>Team members report to two bosses; the Project Manager and the Functional Manager</li><li>Three Matrix types: Strong, Balanced, and Weak</li></ul>

Understand Project Environments: Major considerations in this area that impact the Risk Management Process include understanding of:

a. **Cultural and Social Environment:** Recognize how the project affects people and how people affect the project. Risk that stakeholders will not buy-in to overall project goals increases if this environment is not addressed.

b. **International and Political Environment:** Be familiar with applicable laws and understand current political climates.

c. **Physical Environment:** Understand how the project will impact or be impacted by the surrounding physical environment.

Activity 9A: PMBOK Chapter 1 through 4 Review

Read the eight true or false questions below. Answers are in Appendix A.

Question	True or False
1. All change requests should be listed on a master Issues Log that supports the project.	
2. The Monitoring and Controlling Process Group follows the Planning Process Group.	
3. Configuration Management focuses on controlling changes to the project's product or service's functional and physical characteristics.	
4. Team members may be obligated to report to two managers in a Matrix organizational model.	
5. The focus of the Functional organizational model is on projects.	
6. Silo is a term often associated with the Matrix organizational model.	
7. Stakeholders are refusing to buy-in to overall project goals. In all likelihood, more time should have been spent on the Cultural and Social Environment.	
8. The PMI Framework consists of six interrelated Process Groups, beginning with Initiating and ending with Closing.	

Project Scope Management

It is important to understand the concept of the Scope Baseline and Scope Creep from Chapter 5 of the *PMBOK*.

Scope Baseline: The *Scope Baseline* is a key input that supports many risk management activities. Remember the three components:

- *Scope Statement*: This is the most defined version of the project's deliverables. The Scope Statement defines the type of project as well. The project may be recurring which makes risk management easier. The project may also introduce many new variables which increase the level of risk management difficulty.

- *Work Breakdown Structure (WBS)*: The WBS lists project activities and work packages that must be accomplished to complete the project. The WBS may require updating to reflect additional work required for risk responses. Using the WBS as a tool in risk management allows identification and tracking of risks at the summary, control account, and work package levels.

- *Work Breakdown Structure Dictionary*: Lists the attributes of activities and work packages in the WBS.

Scope Creep: *Scope Creep* refers to changes to the project's scope that is not processed through the formal change control process. Individuals who implement Scope Creep are referred to as *Gold Platers*.

Project Time Management

You need to be aware of a number of areas from Chapter 6 of the *PMBOK*. They include:

- Key Documents Generated from Project Time Management

- Estimating Methods

- Buffer Analysis

- Sources of Conflict

Key Documents Generated from Time Management: There are a number of documents completed during Project Time Management that influence the Risk Management Process.

- *Project Schedule Network Diagrams* are produced during Sequence Activities. Network diagrams show key activity dependencies and provide a visual view of potential path convergence issues. They are also a required input for Monte Carlo analysis.

- The *Resource Breakdown Structure* is an output of the Estimate Activity Resources process. This output shows what resources are required for the project. This is an important document used during initial risk identification.

- The *Schedule Baseline* is the primary output of project time management and represents the approved and accepted project schedule. The Schedule Baseline may be adjusted through the project's formal Integrated Change Control process to account for risk.

Estimating Methods: There are three basic types of estimating methods used. Figure 9.3 below provides a brief review of these methods.

Figure 9.3 Estimating Methods

Estimating Type	Key Characteristic
Analogous	<ul><li>Also referred to as Expert or Top Down Estimating</li><li>Best when a project is repeating or recurring</li><li>Requires expertise and knowledge</li><li>Fast—requires only a summary level WBS</li></ul>
Parametric	<ul><li>Objective estimating method</li><li>Uses numeric data. For example: Units × Time Required = Estimate</li><li>Must have accurate numerical data</li></ul>
Bottom Up	<ul><li>Analyzes data at activity or work package level</li><li>Information provided by those doing the work</li><li>Requires time, effort, and detailed WBS</li><li>Best for projects with ambiguity or unknowns</li></ul>

Buffer Analysis: A *buffer* is defined as non-working time added between two activities to account for identified risks. For example: pour concrete, wait two days for the concrete to set, and then begin construction. The buffer in this case is the two day wait. Buffers are used in conjunction with the *Critical Chain Method* when you are aware of constraints before a final project schedule is published.

Sources of Conflict: Remember that the *number one source of conflict encountered is due to scheduling issues.*

Project Quality Management

Project Quality Management is described in Chapter 8 of the *PMBOK*. Quality standards impact the Risk Analysis and Risk Governance domains. The *Quality Management Plan* is an input used to accomplish the Identify Risks process. Remember these key outputs as shown in Figure 9.4:

Figure 9.4 Quality Management Plan

Quality Consideration	Quality Management Plan Entries
Quality Standards	What quality standards are pertinent to this project? How will the team ensure they are met? Examples: • OSHA (Occupational Safety and Health Administration): Safety • ISO 9000: Recommended quality standards • Sarbanes-Oxley • Industry Standards and Codes
Responsibilities	Who will help manage project quality? What are their specific responsibilities?
Quality Checklists	What steps must be performed that require specific verification? Quality Checklists support the project.
Quality Metrics	What metrics must be measured? Are the metrics SMART? (Specific, Measurable, Accountable, Realistic, Timely)
Targets	What are current performance levels that must be improved upon by this project?

Process Improvement Plan	How will waste and non-value activity be identified and reported?
Quality Assurance	What standards will be checked to prevent problems? How will changes and preventative actions be addressed?
Quality Control	How will inspections be managed? What will be measured and reported? How will changes and corrective actions be addressed?

Activity 9B: Project Scope, Time, and Quality Management Review

Directions: There are key definitions and concepts discussed in *PMBOK* Chapters 5 (Scope), 6 (Time), and 8 (Quality). Match the definition to the responses provided. Answers are in Appendix A.

Scope, Time, and Quality Management Definition and Concept Activity	Response
1. Estimation method used when exact units and time requirements are known.	
2. Defines attributes of project activities and work packages.	
3. The approved and accepted project's start and finish times.	
4. Adding additional functionality through informal channels.	
5. Estimation method that requires a detailed WBS. Analyzes risks at the work package level.	
6. The detailed description of project objectives. Describes critical assumptions and constraints.	
7. A formal or informal plan that defines how waste and non-value project activities will be identified and reported.	
8. Sequence Activities output that shows key activity dependencies and path convergence issues.	
9. Non-working time added to a project schedule between activities to account for risk factors.	
10. Type of estimation based on expert knowledge. Best for repeating-type projects.	
11. Allows for identification and tracking of risks at the summary, control account, and work package levels.	
12. The number one documented source of conflict.	
13. Displays the resources required for a project to include people, supplies, materials, and equipment.	
14. Risk Management Process input that describes project targets, metrics, checklists, and process improvement objectives.	
15. Consists of the WBS, WBS Dictionary, and Scope Statement.	

16. Used to develop a schedule when constraints are known ahead of time that must be addressed.	
17. Individuals or groups responsible for adding additional functionality through informal channels.	
18. Key concepts that dictate project activities. Examples include OSHA and Sarbanes-Oxley.	

Activity 9B: Choose from the following:

    A. Scope Baseline

    B. Scope Statement

    C. WBS

    D. WBS Dictionary

    E. Scope Creep

    F. Gold Platers

    G. Project Network Diagrams

    H. Resource Breakdown Structure

    I. Schedule Baseline

    J. Analogous Estimating

    K. Parametric Estimating

    L. Bottom Up Estimating

    M. Buffers

    N. Critical Chain Method

    O. Quality Management Plan

    P. Quality Standards

    Q. Process Improvement Plan

    R. Schedules

Project Human Resource Management

There are a number of pertinent topics covered in Chapter 9 of the *PMBOK* under Project Human Resource Management. They include:

- Motivational Theories
- Leadership Styles
- Leadership Style Applicability
- Negotiation Methods

Motivational Theories: Motivation impacts stakeholder attitudes. Be aware of the following motivational theories in Figure 9.5 and the individuals responsible for each when applicable.

Figure 9.5 Motivational Theories

Motivational Theory	Key Points
Expectancy Theory	Employees believe effort leads to performance. Performance should be rewarded based on individual expectations. Rewards promote further productivity.
McGregor's Theory X and Y	All workers fit into 1 of 2 groups. Theory X managers believe people are not to be trusted and must be watched. Theory Y managers believe people should be trusted, want to achieve success, and are self–directed.
Maslow's Hierarchy of Needs Theory	Maslow stated that motivation occurs in a hierarchal manner. Each level must be attained before moving to the next. (Physiological – Safety – Social – Esteem – Self Actualization)
Achievement Motivation Theory (Three Needs Theory)	Motivational model developed by David McClelland. States people are motivated by some combination of achievement, affiliation, and empowerment
Hertzberg's Theory	There are hygiene factors and motivating agents. Hygiene factors such as salary, working conditions, benefits, etc. destroy motivation. They do not increase motivation. Motivating factors such as responsibility, growth, and achievement are those that increase motivation.

Leadership Styles: Leadership styles also impact stakeholder support of the Risk Management Process. Figure 9.6 lists various leadership styles. Each style must be used on a situational basis.

Figure 9.6 Leadership Styles

Leadership Style	Definition
Directive	Tell people what to do.
Facilitative	Coordinate and solicit the input of others. A good Project Manager is facilitative.
Coaching	Train and instruct others on how to perform the work.
Supporting	Provide assistance and support as needed to achieve project goals.
Consensus Building	Solve problems based on group input. Strive for decision buy in and agreement.
Consultative	Invite others to provide input and ideas.
Autocratic	Make decisions without input from others.

Tuckman Model: Teams go through a step-by-step growth process. The Tuckman Model is a common five-step model used to depict growth of a team from the moment it is formed. This model is used to determine appropriate situation leadership styles and is outlined in Figure 9.7.

Figure 9.7 Tuckman Model

Stage	Characteristics
Forming	Team meets and learns about the project. Roles are discussed. Expect hesitancy, confusion, anxiety, lack of purpose, and lack of identity. Productivity is low. Best strategy: Tell.
Storming	Team begins to address work, technical decisions, and project management approaches. Conflict can occur which may disrupt the team. Leadership is challenged, cliques form, etc. Productivity decreases. Best strategy: Sell.
Norming	Team members begin to work together. They adjust individual habits to accommodate the team. There is open communication, purpose, confidence, motivation, etc. Productivity improves. Best strategy: Participate.
Performing	Teams are independent, self-directed, and work through issues quickly. There is pride and trust. Productivity peaks. Best strategy: Delegate.
Adjourning	Team completes all work and moves on.

Leadership Style Applicability: Each leadership style can be used to support a variety of situations. Figure 9.8 provides common situations and recommended leadership styles.

Figure 9.8 Situational Leadership Recommendations

Situation	Best Leadership Style
Team is forming and new. They need direction and task oriented information.	Directive, Coaching
Team is storming. There is much conflict, frustration, and confusion.	Facilitative, Consensus Building, Consultative
A decision must be made quickly. Time is of the essence. There is little time for input.	Autocratic
The team is well established and skilled. They are in the norm or perform stages.	Supporting or Laissez-Faire (Hands off management style)

Negotiation: This is one of the Project Manager's key interpersonal skills. Use this in conjunction with influencing. Here are some important points:

- *Functional Manager* is the term associated with managers who own the project human resources needed. The Project Manager must negotiate with the Functional Manager to attain resources and support. Functional Managers may not always be "willing" providers. There are normally competing projects in an organization.

- The ability to influence multiple stakeholders to attain support for the project Risk Management Plan is important. Note these tips for effective negotiating in Figure 9.9.

Figure 9.9 Tips for Effective Negotiating

Tips to Negotiate with Stakeholders
Understand and be able to explain the needs of the project. Be able to specifically spell out "what, why, who, where, when, and how factors" impacting project risk.
Be able to explain the business need for the project in an effort to gain support. The Functional Manager may not recognize project risks, benefits, etc.
Understand that key stakeholders have other jobs to do. Understand their work situations. Be realistic.
Build a relationship. Find out how to assist the stakeholder and create a win-win situation surrounding the need for their support.
Be willing to compromise. Be flexible.

Project Communications Management

A number of areas are pertinent from Chapter 10 of the *PMBOK* under Project Communications Management. They include:

- The Communications Management Plan

- Calculating Communications Channels

- The Communications Model

- Lessons Learned

The Communications Management Plan: The Communications Management Plan is a key document that supports the Risk Management Process. The Communications Management Plan should define who needs to receive risk related communications to include information, responses, status, meetings, etc. Contents should include:

1. **What:** What information needs to be communicated?

2. **Who:** Who must we communicate with? Who owns the communications item? Who authorizes communications? Address stakeholder communications requirements, including who will receive information, and who is responsible to ensure information is communicated.

3. **Why:** Why is the communication important? Why should the receiver care about the communication? What is the value proposition?

4. **How:** What media, methods, language, and technology will be used to communicate? Are there templates, formats, etc.? How will version control be addressed? Flowcharts of the process may be included for clarity.

5. **When and Where:** When should communication occur? What is the optimal frequency for communications? Where will the communications occur?

Communications Channels: Remember how to calculate the number of communications channels. The formula is defined in Figure 9.10 below:

Figure 9.10 Calculating Communications Channels

> **Communications Channels = n(n-1)/2**
>
> **If there are 8 stakeholders**
>
> **8(8-1)/2 = 28 channels**

In this instance, 28 different channels of communications exist. In other words, there are potentially 28 different interpretations of a key project item. The Project Manager must maintain control of communications! The Project Manager's goal is to filter rumors, provide, and maintain the reality of the project.

Communications Model: Understand the communications model shown in Figure 9.11.

Figure 9.11 Communications Model

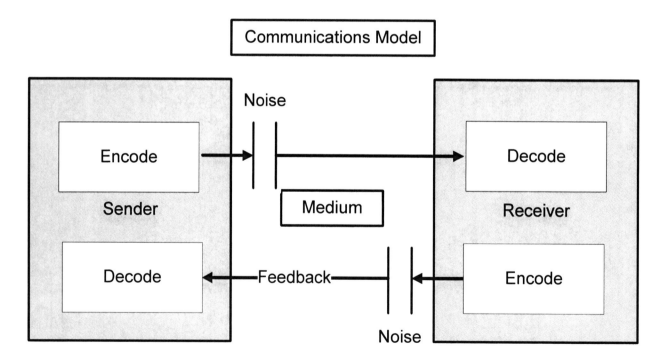

- The sender is responsible to **encode** the message and selects the proper **medium** to get it to the receiver. Examples include e-mail, fax, face-to-face, etc. The sender may use a number of communications methods or technology to encode.

- The receiver is responsible to **decode** the message and selects the proper **medium** to provide feedback. The receiver may use a number of communications methods or technology to decode.

- **Feedback** is the primary output of encoding.

- **Noise** factors may distort and interfere with understanding, transmission, or block the message. PMI refers to noise as *communications blockers*. The goal of communications management is to overcome noise factors to enhance the flow of communication. *The most likely result of noise (communications blockers) is conflict.*

Lessons Learned: *The primary purpose of Lessons Learned is to help future Project Managers improve performance.* Lessons Learned should be accomplished at the end of each project phase. Lessons Learned are sometimes referred to as the "Post Mortem". Lessons Learned support the Risk Management Process as follows:

- Provide past risk communication Lessons Learned and provide ideas to improve risk communications on future projects.

- Improve risk analysis on future projects through review of Lessons Learned.

  o You will save future Project Teams countless hours of research and reduce assumptions.

- Review past risk responses and Contingency Plans. Evaluate what went well, what can be done better, and implement improvement ideas.

  o Conduct Lessons Learned as soon as possible at the completion of a phase or a project. This is when experiences are freshest in the team's mind.

- Refine risk policies and practices to improve risk management effectiveness.

  o Project Management Offices often collect Lessons Learned and incorporate best practices into future Risk Governance policies and procedures.

Activity 9C: Project Human Resource and Communications Management Review

Read the twelve true or false questions below. Answers are in Appendix A.

Question	True or False
1. A Theory X manager is one who believes people should be trusted and are self-directed.	
2. David McClelland is responsible for developing the Achievement Motivation Theory.	
3. According to Hertzberg's Theory, salary is a hygiene factor and responsibility is a motivating agent.	
4. Maslow created the Hierarchy of Needs Theory which places Esteem on the top rung.	
5. Training and instructing others is an attribute of the Consensus Building leadership style.	
6. Autocratic leaders generally make decisions with little or no input from others.	
7. A team entered the Storming phase. Facilitative and Consensus Building leadership styles are optimal in this phase.	
8. Performing is normally a step that a team achieves prior to Norming.	
9. A Functional Manager is a stakeholder who authorizes the Project Manager.	
10. A Project Manager should spend up to 90% of his or her time communicating.	
11. A Communications Management Plan should list key stakeholders who should receive risk related information.	
12. The primary purpose of Lessons Learned is to let stakeholders know how the current project is progressing.	

Project Stakeholder Management

A number of areas are pertinent from Chapter 13 of the *PMBOK* under Project Stakeholder Management. Domain 2 lists a number of key Stakeholder Engagement tasks you need to understand. Many of the areas in Domain 2 are addressed in Chapter 13. Figure 9.12 provides an overview of the four processes in Chapter 13.

Figure 9.12 Project Stakeholder Management

Process	Goal	Major Deliverables
13.1 Identify Stakeholders (Who are the stakeholders? Where are they today, in terms of commitment?)	• Identify stakeholders on the project • Identify Impact—can use the Power/Interest Model	• Initial Stakeholder Register with Stakeholders classified—where they are on the grid?
13.2 Plan Stakeholder Management (Based on where the stakeholders are—and how we move them?)	• Use Stakeholder Management Plan to further classify stakeholders • Model uses Unaware, Resistant, Neutral, Supportive, Leading • Develop a plan of attack to go from current state to desired state	• Stakeholder Management Plan—where are our stakeholders today—and where do they need to be moved to? Define current versus desired state.
13.3 Manage Stakeholder Engagement (Let's move the stakeholders—implement our plan and look for issues)	• Use the Stakeholder Management Plan • Develop and Implement strategies to move from current to desired	• Communications • Issues Management • Creation of an Issues Log used to track stakeholder issues
13.4 Control Stakeholder Engagement (Is everything working? Don't take your eye off the game. Adjust as needed)	• Monitor and control all stakeholder activities • Manage issues to conclusion • Be aware that stakeholder management is a moving target	• Communications • Resolved Issues • Change/Update Stakeholder Register, Stakeholder Management Plan as needed

Stakeholder engagement is critical from the beginning to end of a project. Here are some key tips that support Domain 2 of the PMI-RMP Exam Content Outline:

- **Interpersonal Skills:** Your interpersonal skills will be used to the maximum extent to foster appropriate levels of shared accountability, responsibility, and risk ownership. PMI provides a robust list of 11 interpersonal skills we recommend you perfect to the maximum extent possible. Figure 9.13 lists these skills. They include:

Figure 9.13 Interpersonal Skills

Skill
Effective Communication: Understand communications channels, informational requirements, and be effective
Leadership: Focus efforts of the group toward a common goal. Get things done through others
Coaching: Sharing talents, skills, competencies etc. with others
Motivation: Create environment to meet project objectives and offer self-satisfaction
Conflict Management: Handle, control, and guide to achieve resolution
Negotiation: Confer with concerned parties to make agreements acceptable to all
Political and Cultural Awareness: Use politics and power skillfully to achieve project objectives
Influencing: Share power; get others to cooperate toward common goals
Decision Making: Apply right style to ensure effective decisions are made in a timely manner
Team Building: Help individuals bound by common purpose work with each other and independently
Trust Building: Help people to develop mutual respect, openness, understanding, and empathy, to develop communication and teamwork

- **Foster Engagement:** Include stakeholders in the initial planning meetings to discuss risk. Continue to include them as the project progresses. Share your methodology, stakeholder expectations, and solicit feedback. The best risk management function is one that is owned by the stakeholders and managed by the Project Manager.

- **Train the Trainer:** A Project Manager needs to use his or her Core Team to the maximum extent. Develop the Risk Management Plan, Risk Register, and perform overall risk management as a team. When possible, delegate responsibility. We discussed the concept of a Risk Owner. Use this concept to provide an opportunity for others to own and manage a portion of the overall risk management program. The more your team understands risk management, the greater the chance for the project to succeed. Here is another "PMI-ISM"—*a solid risk management program increases the chances of project success by 90%*. Know this—it may show up on the test!

- **Use the Stakeholder Register:** You need to identify key stakeholders who can influence the project. A key aspect of solid project management is identifying stakeholders, defining their expectations, and managing those expectations. Determine whose tolerance levels matter. Then use your Communications Management Plan to set up meetings, interviews, etc. to determine expectations, and manage them.

- **Use the Stakeholder Management Plan:** Identifying attitudes toward risk, but on a broader basis, the project as a whole is critical. The Stakeholder Management Plan is a tool you can use to determine current attitudes, determine desired attitudes, and develop strategies you can use both guide attitudes in the direction you need them, and manage stakeholder expectations effectively.

- **Probability × Impact = Risk Score**: We discussed this key concept in Chapter 4. All risks are not created equally. Ensure risk prioritization takes into consideration the many views of stakeholders impacted by risk. You may have a team member who believes a risk has an impact rating of 2. Another may believe it is a 5. First, facilitate a discussion. Bring the parties together to share their views. In the end, best practice is to use the higher score moving forward. If possible, have the team member who believes the impact score is higher assume duties as a Risk Owner!

- **Share Responses:** We discussed risk responses in Chapter 6. Make it a practice to have Risk Owners validate proposed responses with stakeholders most likely to be impacted by a risk. Allow the stakeholders to weigh in, and modify the response as necessary. The best risk responses are those where across the board buy-in to the maximum extent is received.

- **Roles and Responsibilities:** Explain and define the role of Risk Owner. Encourage team members and stakeholders to step up and volunteer for the role. Solicit help of experienced Risk Owners to help and train newly assigned Risk Owners. Here's another PMI-ISM-your number one power as a Project Manager is reward power. If someone excels, call them out in a positive way.

- **A Waterfall Scrum of Scrums:** In Scrum, ScrumMasters from each team periodically meet together to compare status, issues, Lessons Learned, etc. Oftentimes, Project A may impact Projects B, C, etc. These dependencies or interrelationships present risks that need to be identified and analyzed. Periodically identify projects impacting your project, meet with fellow Project Managers, and manage risk before it manages you!

Project Stakeholder Management: Key Concepts

A *Stakeholder Register* identifies stakeholders for the project. This document should be completed by the Project Manager and shared with all stakeholders to ensure understanding and commitment. The Stakeholder Register should have a comments section you can use for multiple purposes. Some comments may be simple clarifications of roles. Other pertinent comments may spell out specific expectations. Risk may very well be an expectation you feel the need to share. Here is an example of a Stakeholder Register. Figure 9.14 shares a template I developed. Note this template is not a PMI standard.

Figure 9.14: Stakeholder Register

Stakeholder Register							
Stakeholder Segment:							
Name	Organization	Role	R	A	C	I	Comments

RACI Terms Defined	R	Responsible for doing work on the project
	A	Accountable for outcomes
	C	Consult as Subject Matter Expert
	I	Inform as the project progresses

Version:

A Stakeholder Management Plan identifies key stakeholders for the project. This document should also be completed by the Project Manager. However, this is a document not meant for wide distribution. It is managed by the Project Manager and shared with select team members only. Note the Stakeholder Management Plan in Figure 9.15 lists key stakeholders and categorizes them based on five Level of Commitment designators. The goal of the plan is to determine current states, determine desired states, and develop strategies to move stakeholders from current to desired states. This plan can be used to develop strategies for stakeholders to ensure everyone is moving in the right direction and supportive or leading risk management efforts.

Figure 9.15 Stakeholder Management Plan

Stakeholder Management Plan			
Name	Current State	Desired State	Strategy

Recommended Level of Commitment Designators		
	U	Unaware: Stakeholder is unaware of the project.
	N	Neutral: Stakeholder has yet to determine level of support.
	R	Resistant: Stakeholder does not support the project.
	S	Supportive: Stakeholder agrees with the project.
	L	Leading: Stakeholder is supportive and actively engaged in project.

Activity 9D: Project Stakeholder Management Review

Review the scenarios. Match the scenario to the correct Stakeholder Management process.

Scenario	Stakeholder Management Process Group
1. A member of the Core Team developed an issue log that will be used to determine where stakeholder engagement levels are currently. This issue log is dependent upon the Stakeholder Management Plan, Communications Management Plan, and the Integrated Change Control Log.	
2. A key stakeholder is currently unaware of key project details. The Project Manager evaluated this stakeholder and determined she needs to be supportive for the project to succeed. The Project Manager developed a strategy targeting this stakeholder to bring her to the desired engagement level.	
3. A Project Manager is reviewing the Stakeholder Management Plan to determine the strategy being used to achieve a desired engagement level of Leading for a key organizational decision maker. He determines the strategy currently being employed is not effective and adjusts his approach.	
4. A Project Manager just completed a review of a potential project and is trying to identify which stakeholders are impacted. She plans to both identify stakeholders and determine their current level of commitment using an influence and impact assessment.	
5. The project team is reviewing stakeholder issues and Work Performance Data generated over the past three-months and developing Lessons Learned. The information will be analyzed and used to provide pertinent Work Performance Information for the next Work Performance Report.	
6. A number of issues developed that the project team must now address. They determined that key skills such as influencing and negotiation are critical to success. In addition, knowledge of finance will be critical as a key stakeholder questioned the economic value of the project.	

Scenario	Stakeholder Management Process Group
7. A Project Manager reviewed a recently completed Stakeholder Register and developed a highly sensitive plan that lists desired engagement levels, and provides a tailored strategy for each key stakeholder ensure the desired engagement level is achieved. This process required a number of Meetings and extensive use of Analytical Techniques.	
8. A Project Manager just completed a comprehensive Brainstorming session with potential project stakeholders to determine who he should collaborate with regarding the project he was recently assigned. He plans to follow up this Brainstorming session with a few interviews of who he believes are key stakeholders to validate their interest and impact.	

Risk Management Process Outputs: Impact other Areas of Project Management

Outputs of the Risk Management Process are key inputs to other key activities that support a project. Figure 9.16 shows the risk output, where it acts as an input, and the significance of this relationship.

Figure 9.16 Output of Risk Management Processes

Risk Management Output	Acts as Input To	Significance
Risk Register	Estimate Activity Resources Estimate Activity Durations Develop Schedule Chapter 6	Considers impact of risk key aspects of project schedule development.
Risk Register	Estimate Costs Determine Budget *PMBOK* Chapter 7	Considers impact of risk on project cost estimating and project budget development.

Risk Register	Plan Quality Management *PMBOK* Chapter 8	Considers impact of risks on performance metrics, targets, Quality Assurance, and Quality Control.
Risk Register	Plan Procurement Management *PMBOK* Chapter 12	Considers impact of risk on end-to-end procurement process.

APPENDIX A: Activity Solutions

Activity 1: Risk Management Process

Question	True or False
1. Project risk is normally highest during the project Executing Process Group.	False. Risk is highest during the Initiating Process Group.
2. The first step in the Risk Management Process is Identify Risks.	False. The first step is Plan Risk Management.
3. The Plan Risk Responses process occurs in the Project Planning Process Group.	True. The first five processes in the Project Risk Management occur in Project Planning.
4. Three of the most common constraints that determine stakeholder tolerance levels include scope, resources, and stakeholder expectations.	False. Stakeholder expectations are not one of the Seven Constraints.
5. The Project Manager must attempt to attain an organizational commitment to the value of risk management.	True. This can make or break the potential for a successful risk management function.
6. Management Reserves are defined as reserves to address unknown risks.	True. This is a correct definition.
7. A risk that is identified early in the Risk Management Process is called an Emergent Risk.	False. Emergent Risks are those identified as the project progresses.
8. The Perform Quantitative Risk Analysis process is mandatory. It is a subjective analysis method.	False. The Perform Quantitative Risk Analysis process is optional and depends on the project. It is an objective analysis method.
9. Stakeholder risk attitudes and tolerances can impact overall risk prioritization and response efforts.	True. Attitudes and tolerances can also impact the amount of reserves available as well.
10. The Risk Register is developed as part of the Plan Risk Management process of Project Risk Management.	False. It is developed during the Identify Risks process.
11. Insurable, or Pure Risks, can be both negative and positive.	False. Insurable, or Pure Risks, are always negative.
12. When a positive risk occurs, it is referred to as a benefit.	True. Negative risks that occur are referred to as issues. Positive risks that occur are referred to as benefits.

Activity 2: Plan Risk Management Process

Plan Risk Management Definition and Concept Activity	Response
1. A tool and technique used in the Plan Risk Management process that encourages you to seek the help of multiple stakeholders when planning risk.	G
2. A term that describes a measure of the amount or range of risk a stakeholder is willing to tolerate.	C
3. A practice that allows for identification of risks with common causes that normally leads to more effective responses.	B
4. Any factor that can limit the team's options. Boundaries that must be addressed and planned.	H
5. A key deliverable that defines the overall strategy to be used to support the project's end-to-end Risk Management Process.	E
6. Key input to the Plan Risk Management process. Includes Lessons Learned, stakeholder tolerance information, templates, policies, and/or procedures.	A
7. A tool that provides a hierarchical breakout of potential risks by category. Shows potential risks and risk thresholds for risks within each category.	F
8. Something the team believes to be true but has not yet validated.	D
9. Areas where key stakeholders are willing to accept risk.	I
10. A key input to the Plan Risk management process that defines key stakeholders, their roles, and the current commitment level they possess.	J
11. Conditions not under the immediate control of the team. A common process input. Specifically culture, systems, and values.	K
12. Term that describes a person or organization's willingness to accept risk.	L

Activity 2: Choose from the following:

A. Organizational Process Assets

B. Categorization

C. Risk Threshold

D. Assumption

E. Risk Management Plan

F. Risk Breakdown Structure (RBS)

G. Expert Judgement

H. Constraints

I. Risk Tolerance Areas

J. Stakeholder Register

K. Enterprise Environmental Factors

L. Risk Utility

Activity 3: Identify Risks Process

Question	True or False
1. The Identify Risks process produces the final iteration of the Risk Register.	False. This is the initial Risk Register, which will be updated in later steps.
2. Checklist Analysis is a fast and efficient means of identifying new risks missed during the initial review.	False. Checklist Analysis is quick. However, it does not identify risks not on the checklist.
3. Another term for Delphi Technique is Social Intelligence. It allows experts to review the final results and provide additional feedback.	True. Delphi Technique provides Social Intelligence and the consensus of the group.
4. SWOT analysis is a practical means to gather information from a group of selected stakeholders and rank order the inputs.	False. This is a great definition for Nominal Group Technique.
5. The Stakeholder Register provides a strategy for managing stakeholder expectations.	False. The Stakeholder Management Strategy provides instructions to manage expectations.
6. The worst thing to do during a Brainstorming session is to evaluate participant responses.	True. All responses should be documented without analysis to ensure success.
7. The Risk Register should have restricted access and not be made available to all project stakeholders.	False. The Risk Register should be shared and visible to all key stakeholders.
8. The Risk Register is an essential input that will allow for development of a comprehensive Risk Management Plan.	False. The Risk Management Plan is an input from the Plan Risk Management process that facilitates development of a Risk Register.
9. Roles and responsibilities supporting the Identify Risks process are defined during the Plan Risk Management process.	True. Roles and responsibilities are part of the Risk Management Plan.
10. Emergent Risks should be added to the Risk Register.	True. Add Emergent Risks as soon as identified.
11. It is best to identify risks at the conclusion of all other project planning activities.	False. Identify risks as early as possible in the planning process. Give your team time to generate responses.
12. Identify Risks process tools and techniques include tools that look into the past, present, and future.	True. All tools and techniques fall under these three categories.

Activity 4: Perform Qualitative Risk Analysis

Perform Qualitative Risk Analysis Definition and Concept Activity	Response
1. The product of multiplying probability times impact.	H
2. A situation where multiple activities feed into a single activity. Increases risk.	A
3. A numeric value that shows how an individual Risk Score compares with other individual Risk Scores.	I
4. The chances that a risk event may occur.	M
5. A list of risks determined to be very high priority.	D
6. Term that defines the level of risk on a project as defined by the Project Risk Score.	E
7. Situation where stakeholder Risk Ratings and Risk Scores are impacted by perceptions.	K
8. The two most effective ways to accomplish the Perform Qualitative Risk Analysis process.	B
9. The cumulative value of all Risk Scores.	G
10. A key planning tool that must be updated at the completion of the Perform Qualitative Risk Analysis process.	O
11. A key input that facilitates performance of the Perform Qualitative Risk Analysis process.	P
12. Situation occurs when stakeholders intentionally try to manipulate and impact Risk Ratings and Risk Scores.	J
13. A list of risks determined to be a lower priority than others.	C

14. The numeric values assigned to show the probability and impact of a risk event.	F
15. Standard Probability and Risk Matrix that shows ratings and overall priority determinations.	L
16. A numeric Risk Rating that expresses the consequences to a project if a risk occurs.	N

Activity 4: Choose from the following:

A. Path Convergence

B. Meetings and Interviews

C. Watch List

D. Urgent List

E. Risk Exposure

F. Risk Rating

G. Project Risk Score

H. Risk Score

I. Risk Rating within Project

J. Motivational Bias

K. Cognitive Bias

L. Lookup Table

M. Probability

N. Impact

O. Risk Register

P. Scope Baseline

Activity 5: Perform Quantitative Risk Analysis

Part I: Three Point Estimating

Three estimates are given. Calculate the best estimate using Three Point Averaging and Three Point PERT. Then calculate the Standard Deviation.

Estimate to Complete Activity	Number of Days Estimated
Pessimistic	28 Days
Most Likely	12 Days
Optimistic	8 Days

Three Point Averaging	16
PERT	14
Standard Deviation	3.33

Part II: EMV

Five risks impacting your project are identified as follows. How much in total Contingency Reserves should be requested?

RISK	PROBABILITY	IMPACT	EMV
A	10%	($20,000)	($2,000)
B	40%	$30,000	$12,000
C	30%	$27,000	$8,100
D	50%	$18,000	$9,000
E	25%	$44,000	$11,000
TOTAL			$38,100

Risk D occurs. How much remains in the Contingency Reserves? *(Impact is $18,000)*

$38,100 - $18,000 = $20,100

Part III: Monte Carlo Analysis

What is the probability of achieving a goal of spending $40M?

40%

The organization wants to have an 80% probability of achieving cost objectives. What is the cost to achieve 80%?

$80M

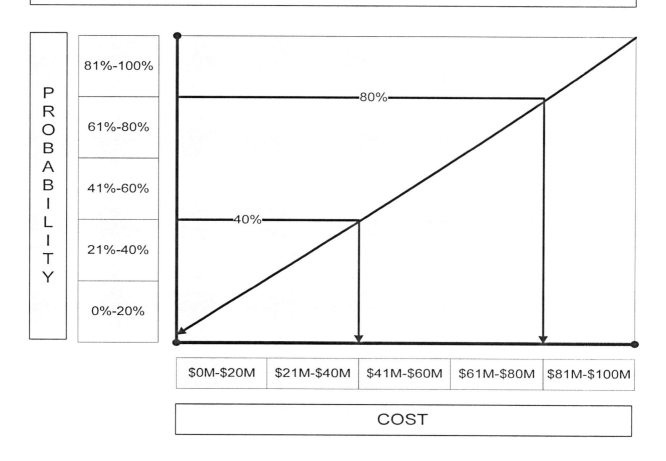

Part IV: Decision Tree Analysis

What is the EMV of the Make decision?

$$((.4 \times \$80) + (.6 \times \$40)) - \$50M = \$6M$$

What is the EMV of the Buy decision?

$$((.4 \times \$70) + (.6 \times \$20)) - \$30M = \$10M$$

What is the best decision based on EMV?

Buy Decision has best EMV

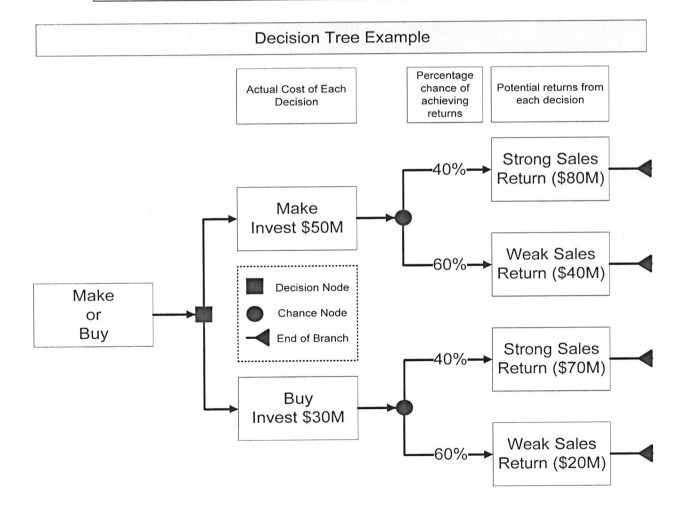

Part V: Tools and Techniques Match Game

Match the tool and technique definition to the correct response.

Perform Quantitative Risk Analysis Tool and Technique Search Activity	Response
1. Any technique for creating images, diagrams, or animations to communicate a message.	J
2. Analysis method that uses several What If scenarios to calculate potential results. Modeling technique that helps determine which risks have the greatest impact on a project.	C
3. Method used widely to establish Contingency Reserve requirements for both budget and schedule. Quantified by multiplying probability times the best or worst case cost/time scenario.	G
4. Simulation technique that furnishes the decision-maker with a range of possible outcomes and the probabilities they will occur for any choice of action.	F
5. A bar graph that shows the best case and worst case cost or benefit scenario for a risk.	D
6. Defines accelerators that can move a project toward a successful conclusion, and resistors that can move a project toward an unsuccessful conclusion.	L
7. Technique includes a mix of open-ended and prepared questions. Begin with open-ended questions to gain insight from the interviewer. Follow up with prepared questions.	A
8. Looks at potential scenarios that may impact a project and determines risk factors for each scenario.	I
9. Provides a comprehensive, hierarchical and rational framework for structuring a decision problem, for representing and quantifying its elements, for relating those elements to overall goals, and for evaluating alternative solutions.	E
10. Estimates the potential of a risk event to occur over a pre-described range, generally over a normal distribution.	B
11. Analyzes scenarios by opening perspectives beyond immediate constraints. Enhances the capacity of policy-makers and practitioners to anticipate change, grasp opportunities, and cope with threats.	K
12. Describes a scenario under consideration and uses available data to determine the most economic approach. The primary objective is selecting the scenario that provides the best overall Expected Monetary Value (EMV).	H

Activity V: Choose from the following:

A. Interviewing

B. Probability Distribution

C. Sensitivity Analysis

D. Tornado Diagram

E. Analytical Hierarchy Process

F. Monte Carlo Technique

G. Expected Monetary Value (EMV)

H. Decision Tree Analysis

I. Scenario Planning

J. Visualization

K. Futures Thinking

L. Force Field Analysis

Activity 6: Plan Risk Responses

Scenario	Response Being Used
1. You determine a planned feature is not technically feasible. You eliminate the feature from the Project Scope.	Avoid
2. You can get a 10% discount from a key supplier if you order 100,000 units. Your project requires 80,000 units. You contact other Project Managers to determine if there are needs for the additional units to gain the discount.	Share
3. There is an opportunity to save over $10,000 if you accept a seller's offer. Your team agrees the offer is good but determines not to pursue it at this time.	Accept
4. You learn of an opportunity to cut three weeks off your project schedule. Resources are available that allow you to crash key critical activities to increase the probability of achieving the time savings.	Enhance
5. You learn that a competitor is attempting to replicate one of your key products. You add additional technical features that cannot be duplicated that will prevent the competitor from building a like product.	Avoid
6. You add incentives to increase the probability of early completion of a key work package by a critical vendor.	Enhance
7. Your team does not have the expertise to eliminate a key safety risk. You spend $10,000 to enlist the support of a third-party vendor who will respond to the risk.	Transfer
8. You learn that a new external regulation was discovered that adds risk to completing your project within budget. You determine that you will deal with any risks that materialize when they occur.	Accept
9. A new Project Manager heard there is a risk response that can be used to address both positive and negative risks.	Accept
10. There are two key risks to your project schedule. You develop a training program to respond to the first. For the second risk, you develop a prototype that will enhance testing.	Mitigate
11. You develop some Teaming Agreements with a key supplier to improve levels of cooperation and improve Return on Investment.	Share
12. You are told there are four potential responses to address negative risks or threats. You remember Accept, Transfer, and Avoid. Which did you miss?	Mitigate
13. You add an additional vendor at a cost of $25,000 with the expertise to ensure an identified risk event occurs that will lead to opportunities to reduce time spent on critical path activities.	Exploit

Activity 7: Control Risks Concepts

Control Risks Definition and Concept Activity	Response
1. Provides reserves to support risks identified on the Risk Register.	H
2. Examines and documents the effectiveness of risk responses and the overall Risk Management Process.	B
3. Risks that may result directly from implementing a planned Contingency Plan.	E
4. Provides funds to support Emergent Risks.	G
5. May be required to request additional reserves for a newly identified risk response.	F
6. Part of a Risk Reassessment that may include changing the order or priority of risks, adjusting the severity of existing risks, or monitoring Residual Risks.	A
7. Risks that remain after implementing a planned Risk Response Plan. They must be accounted for on the Risk Register.	D
8. Compares project technical accomplishments to the schedule defining when technical achievement is required.	I
9. A process that identifies new risks, reassesses current risks, and closes out risks that are no longer applicable.	C
10. An output of Control Risks that uses Work Performance Data to compile.	J

Activity 7: Choose from the following:

A. Risk Review

B. Risk Audit

C. Risk Reassessment

D. Residual Risks

E. Secondary Risks

F. Change Requests

G. Management Reserves

H. Contingency Reserves

I. Technical Performance Measurement

J. Work Performance Information

Activity 8: Risk Governance

Statement	True or False
1. Risk Governance is accomplished primarily during the Plan Risk Management process of Project Risk Management.	False. Risk Governance is accomplished primarily in the Control Risks process.
2. ISO is an organization developed to inspect final project deliverables for technical compliance.	False. ISO develops standards that drive success.
3. A $50,000 project is 50% complete. Actual Costs are $30,000. CPI is .83.	True. EV (25K)/AC (30K) = .83.
4. The buyer accepts the Cost Risk for a Cost Reimbursement type of contract.	True.
5. A Cost Plus Percentage of Cost contract poses the lowest level of risk to a buyer.	False. It poses the highest level of risk.
6. Identify Risks is the process of ensuring risk policies and procedures are understood, followed, consistently applied, and effective.	False. This is a definition for Risk Governance.
7. A key Risk Governance activity is the development of metrics to guide organizational risk management activities.	True.
8. Risk Governance is concerned with how policies and procedures are implemented rather than the creation of policies and procedures.	False. Risk Governance creates policies and monitors their implementation.
9. The primary goal of the IRGC is to facilitate understanding and manage risks that impact society, human health, safety, and the environment as a whole.	True
10. Lessons Learned meetings should be limited to discuss solely what went well and what could go better.	False. Always add what can be done better next time.
11. A quick review of your project reveals a CPI of 1.2. You should conclude your project is behind on budget.	False. A CPI of greater than 1.0 indicates a project is ahead on budget.

Activity 9A: PMBOK Chapter 1 through 4 Review

Question	True or False
1. All change requests should be listed on a master Issues Log that supports the project.	False. All change requests should be listed on a Change Control Log. Issues Logs are reserved for risks that became issues or questions that must be answered.
2. The Monitoring and Controlling Process Group follows the Planning Process Group.	False. The Monitoring and Controlling Process Group follows the Executing Process Group.
3. Configuration Management focuses on controlling changes to the project's product or service's functional and physical characteristics.	True. Configuration Management may be added to the project's Integrated Change Control function.
4. Team members may be obligated to report to two managers in a Matrix organizational model.	True. This is a characteristic of the Matrix organizational model.
5. The focus of the Functional organizational model is on projects.	False. Focus on projects is a characteristic of the Projectized organizational model.
6. Silo is a term often associated with the Matrix organizational model.	False. The Silo term is associated with the Functional organizational model.
7. Stakeholders are refusing to buy-in to overall project goals. In all likelihood, more time should have been spent on the Cultural and Social Environment.	True. A failure to achieve stakeholder buy-in normally is indicative of a lack of attention on the Cultural and Social Environment.
8. The PMI Framework consists of six interrelated Process Groups beginning with Initiating and ending with Closing.	False. There are five interrelated Process Groups.

Activity 9B: Project Scope, Time, and Quality Management Review

Scope, Time, and Quality Management Definition and Concept Activity	Response
1. Estimation method used when exact units and time requirements are known.	K
2. Defines attributes of project activities and work packages.	D
3. The approved and accepted project's start and finish times.	I
4. Adding additional functionality through informal channels.	E
5. Estimation method that requires a detailed WBS. Analyzes risks at the work package level.	L
6. The detailed description of project objectives. Describes critical assumptions and constraints.	B
7. A formal or informal plan that defines how waste and non-value project activities will be identified and reported.	Q
8. Sequence Activities output that shows key activity dependencies and path convergence issues.	G
9. Non-working time added to a project schedule between activities to account for risk factors.	M
10. Type of estimation based on expert knowledge. Best for repeating-type projects.	J
11. Allows for identification and tracking of risks at the summary, control account, and work package levels.	C
12. The number one documented source of conflict.	R
13. Displays the resources required for a project to include people, supplies, materials, and equipment.	H
14. Risk Management Process input that describes project targets, metrics, checklists, and process improvement objectives.	O
15. Consists of the WBS, WBS Dictionary, and Scope Statement.	A
16. Used to develop a schedule when constraints are known ahead of time that must be addressed.	N
17. Individuals or groups responsible for adding additional functionality through informal channels.	F
18. Key concepts that dictate project activities. Examples include OSHA and Sarbanes-Oxley.	P

Activity 9B: Choose from the following:

A. Scope Baseline

B. Scope Statement

C. WBS

D. WBS Dictionary

E. Scope Creep

F. Gold Platers

G. Project Network Diagrams

H. Resource Breakdown Structure

I. Schedule Baseline

J. Analogous Estimating

K. Parametric Estimating

L. Bottom Up Estimating

M. Buffers

N. Critical Chain Method

O. Quality Management Plan

P. Quality Standards

Q. Process Improvement Plan

R. Schedules

Activity 9C: Project Human Resource and Communications Management Review

Question	True or False
1. A Theory X manager is one who believes people should be trusted and are self-directed.	False. This definition fits a Theory Y manager.
2. David McClelland is responsible for developing the Achievement Motivation Theory.	True. McClelland states that there are three needs that motivate. They include achievement, affiliation, and power.
3. According to Hertzberg's Theory, salary is a hygiene factor and responsibility is a motivating agent.	True. Salary as a hygiene factor is not agreed upon by many who review Hertzberg's Theory.
4. Maslow created the Hierarchy of Needs Theory which places Esteem on the top rung.	False. Maslow did create the theory. However, Self-Actualization is the top level.
5. Training and instructing others is an attribute of the Consensus Building leadership style.	False. This is an attribute of the Coaching leadership style.
6. Autocratic leaders generally make decisions with little or no input from others.	True. This is an attribute of the Autocratic leadership style.
7. A team entered the Storming phase. Facilitative and Consensus Building leadership styles are optimal in this phase.	True. A third choice in Storming is use of the Consultative leadership style.
8. Performing is normally a step that a team achieves prior to Norming.	False. The steps in the Tuckman Model are Forming, Storming, Norming, Performing and Adjourning.
9. A Functional Manager is a stakeholder who authorizes the Project Manager.	False. A Functional Manager provides human resources for the project.
10. A Project Manager should spend up to 90% of his or her time communicating.	True. Communications is a key to success. 90% is the magic number!
11. A Communications Management Plan should list key stakeholders who should receive risk related information.	True. This is a key reason why the Communications Management Plan is an input to the Plan Risk Management process.
12. The primary purpose of Lessons Learned is to let stakeholders know how the current project is progressing.	False. The primary purpose is to help future Project Managers.

Activity 9D: Project Stakeholder Management Review

Scenario	Stakeholder Management Process Group
1. A member of the Core Team developed an issue log that will be used to determine where stakeholder engagement levels are currently. This issue log is dependent upon the Stakeholder Management Plan, Communications Management Plan, and the Integrated Change Control Log.	Manage Stakeholder Engagement
2. A key stakeholder is currently unaware of key project details. The Project Manager evaluated this stakeholder and determined she needs to be supportive for the project to succeed. The Project Manager developed a strategy targeting this stakeholder to bring her to the desired engagement level.	Plan Stakeholder Management
3. A Project Manager is reviewing the Stakeholder Management Plan to determine the strategy being used to achieve a desired engagement level of Leading for a key organizational decision maker. He determines the strategy currently being employed is not effective and adjusts his approach.	Control Stakeholder Engagement
4. A Project Manager just completed a review of a potential project and is trying to identify which stakeholders are impacted. She plans to both identify stakeholders, and determine their current level of commitment using an influence and impact assessment.	Identify Stakeholders
5. The project team is reviewing stakeholder issues and Work Performance Data generated over the past three-months and developing Lessons Learned. The information will be analyzed and used to provide pertinent Work Performance Information for the next Work Performance Report.	Control Stakeholder Engagement
6. A number of issues developed that the project team must now address. They determined that key skills such as influencing and negotiation are critical to success. In addition, knowledge of finance will be critical as a key stakeholder questioned the economic value of the project.	Manage Stakeholder Engagement

Scenario	Stakeholder Management Process Group
7. A Project Manager reviewed a recently completed Stakeholder Register and developed a highly sensitive plan that lists desired engagement levels, and provides a tailored strategy for each key stakeholder ensure the desired engagement level is achieved. This process required a number of meetings, and extensive use of analytical techniques.	Plan Stakeholder Management
8. A Project Manager just completed a comprehensive Brainstorming session with potential project stakeholders to determine who he should collaborate with regarding the project he was recently assigned to. He plans to follow up this Brainstorming session with a few interviews of who he believes are key stakeholders to validate their interest and impact.	Identify Stakeholders

APPENDIX B: Final 150 Question Test

Congratulations on completing all activities. Are you ready to take a challenging 150 question test that is representative of actual questions that will be encountered on the PMI-RMP test?

Read each question and answer carefully. Answers with explanations are provided at the end of the test. Try to achieve 75%, or approximately 112 questions correct. Take the test again and again until you can reach and achieve this goal or higher. Can you achieve 90% (approximately 135 questions correct)? Go for it!

Question #	Question	Responses	Response
1.	Which of the following statements regarding the Perform Qualitative Risk Analysis process is correct?	a. An objective process that assesses the probabilities and impacts of risks. b. A subjective process that assesses the probability of achieving specific project objectives. c. An objective process that analyzes possible outcomes and probabilities. d. A subjective process that uses a Probability and Impact Matrix.	
2.	You are analyzing reserve requirements for your project. You want to identify reserves for unknown risks you suspect will materialize by the end of the project. What type of reserves do you need to identify?	a. Contingency Reserves b. Expected Monetary Value c. Management Reserves d. Discretionary Reserves	
3.	You are beginning the Plan Risk Management process. What is the first thing you should do?	a. Define Probability and Impact Rating Systems b. List categories of risks c. Set up a planning meeting d. Determine available organizational process assets	

4.	Which of the following areas should be documented in an initial Risk Register?	a. Expected Monetary Value analysis b. Detailed risk responses c. Risk Ratings for all risks d. Risk description and causes	
5.	There are four identified risks. Risk A has a probability (P) of 5 and impact (I) of 2. Risk B has P-3, I-4. Risk C has P-4, I-4. Risk D has P-2, I-5. Which risk has the highest priority?	a. Risk A b. Risk B c. Risk C d. Risk D	
6.	Which of the following statements is correct regarding the Perform Qualitative Risk Analysis process?	a. It addresses individual risks b. It provides an objective analysis c. It is performed when the priority of a project warrants it d. It provides a numerical analysis of cost and schedule probabilities	
7.	A Project Manager should normally spend what percentage of his or her time communicating?	a. 75% b. 82% c. 90% d. 95%	
8.	Analytical Techniques used during risk planning should consider which three key areas of focus?	a. People, Tools, Business b. People, Scope, Business c. Scope, Tools, Business d. People, Tools, Scope	
9.	Four risks are identified for Project XYZ. Probability and impact for each risk are: Risk A: 40% probability with $8,000 impact Risk B: 20% probability with $5,000 impact Risk C: 10% probability with ($10,000) impact Risk D: 80% probability with $6,000 impact What amount of Contingency Reserves is required for this project?	a. ($2,900) b. $8,000 c. ($8,000) d. $10,000	

10.	Use the information from Question 9 above. Risk B occurred. How much Contingency Reserves remain?	a. $2,000 b. $2,400 c. $3,000 d. $7,000	
11.	Your team is established and is working well together. For the most part, they know the work to be done and remain focused. Which leadership style is best suited for this team?	a. Coaching b. Supportive c. Facilitative d. Autocratic	
12.	Which of the following statements regarding risk management is true?	a. Include all stakeholders in risk management and solicit input from multiple sources. b. Support of risk management functions can be expected from all stakeholders based on the priority of risk management. c. Manage each risk. It only takes one risk to destroy a project. d. Anticipate stakeholder's risk tolerance and plan responses accordingly.	
13.	You want to ensure all risks are linked to project objectives. Which objectives should be considered?	a. Time, Cost, Scope, Quality b. Time, Cost, Scope, Communications c. Scope, Communications, Quality, Resources d. Communications, Quality, Resources, Schedules	
14.	Risk is best defined as:	a. An uncertain event that can impact the project negatively b. An uncertain event that can impact at least one project objective c. An unknown event that can impact project objectives d. An uncertain event that occurs during the Project Executing Group	

15.	It is said that a solid risk management program can reduce project problems and issues by as much as:	a. 100% b. 90% c. 80% d. 70%	
16.	Which of the following statements is true regarding a Look Up Table?	a. Part of Enterprise Environmental Factors and documented in the Risk Register b. Part of Organizational Process Assets and documented in the Risk Register c. Part of Enterprise Environmental Factors and documented in the Risk Management Plan d. Part of Organizational Process Assets and documented in the Risk Management Plan	
17.	You want to determine the process and strategy for accomplishing the overall Risk Management Process. Where can this information be found?	a. Risk Register b. Risk Breakdown Structure c. Risk Management Plan d. Stakeholder Register	
18.	A number of Emergent Risks were identified. You listed them in the Risk Register. What is the next logical step?	a. Perform Qualitative Risk Analysis b. Earned Value Analysis c. Perform Quantitative Risk Analysis d. Expected Monetary Value	
19.	What is the BEST reason to categorize risks?	a. Adds structure to the Risk Register b. Allows for development of better responses c. Removes ambiguity and improves clarity d. Satisfies risk metalanguage requirements	

20.	A number of new risks were discovered during execution of a major project deliverable. What should you do first to address these new risks?	a. Add the new risks to the Risk Register. b. Evaluate and qualify the risk immediately to determine follow up actions. c. Develop a response plan and brief all key stakeholders as soon as possible. d. Perform a Risk Audit to determine the potential impact of each risk.	
21.	A Project Manager works in an organization where many resources must come from external groups. At times, he feels he works for two bosses. What organizational model is being described?	a. Functional b. Projectized c. Matrix d. Silo	
22.	You determined that there is a 60% chance a risk may occur during month two of the project. The project is now in its fifth month and a team member asks what the current probability of the risk occurring is now. You should respond as:	a. 30% b. 24% c. Unknown d. 60%	
23.	There are a total of eight stakeholders a project. How many total communications channels exist?	a. 8 b. 28 c. 36 d. 56	
24.	You are told that the optimistic schedule estimate to complete a key activity is 6 days. The most likely scenario is 9 days. The pessimistic estimate is 18 days. Calculate the Standard Deviation for this scenario.	a. 11 b. 6 c. 2 d. 1.5	

25.	You want to ensure that risks are analyzed for all new proposed change requests. What component ensures this will occur?	a. Integrated Change Control b. Configuration Management c. Risk Management Process d. Project Scope Management	
26.	You want to ensure you provide project risk status to the right stakeholder audience. Which plan should you refer to satisfy this objective?	a. Stakeholder Register b. Stakeholder Management Strategy c. Communications Management Plan d. Risk Breakdown Structure	
27.	You are looking at a graph that shows a number of specific events and the frequency in which they occurred. This chart shows how the number of events peaked on the low cost side of the mean. What type of graph are you most likely looking at?	a. Beta Distribution b. Uniform Distribution c. Triangular Distribution d. Normal Distribution	
28.	You completed your Risk Register and are assigning initial Risk Owners. What is the *best* source from which to find appropriate Risk Owners?	a. Team b. Past Project Managers c. Sponsors d. Project Stakeholders	
29.	You identified a new risk as low priority and low impact. You are confident that the Data Quality Assessment supports this Risk Rating. What should be done?	a. Track as a Residual Risk. b. Add the risk to the Watch List. c. Develop a Fallback Plan d. Quantify using Probability × Impact.	
30.	Which of the following areas should be addressed in a Risk Management Plan?	a. Budgeting, timing, tracking, change management b. Budgeting, timing, risk categories, change management c. Budgeting, timing, tracking, risk categories d. Change management, timing, tracking, risk categories	

31.	Part of your governance process is to identify and leverage standards consistent with organizational norms. Where can the standards that impact your project most likely be found?	a. Quality Management Plan b. Scope Baseline c. Risk Management Plan d. Stakeholder Register	
32.	Pierre needs to solicit ideas from experts located in multiple geographic areas. He plans to use a questionnaire to collect feedback. Which Information Gathering Technique will he use?	a. Root Cause Analysis b. Sensitivity Analysis c. Delphi Technique d. Nominal Group Technique	
33.	You are looking for a tool that defines risk categories and breaks out each category into potential High, Moderate, and Low risks. What tool is being described?	a. Probability and Impact Matrix b. Risk Urgency Assessment c. Risk Register d. Risk Breakdown Structure	
34.	What is an overall term that describes a stakeholder's willingness to accept risk?	a. Risk Averse b. Risk Utility c. Risk Threshold d. Risk Bias	
35.	Risk Metalanguage uses a three-step approach to identify and define risks. This approach includes:	a. Cause, Effect, Cost b. Risk, Effect, Cost c. Cause, Risk, Effect d. Cause, Risk, Cost	
36.	You are reviewing Identify Risk tools and techniques. Which tool and technique requires the most time to complete?	a. Interviews b. Affinity Diagramming c. Delphi Technique d. SWOT	
37.	What key output would you refer to determine the greatest potential for path convergence?	a. WBS b. WBS Dictionary c. Activity Duration Estimates d. Project Network Diagram	

38.	Which tool and technique provides a high-level list of generic categories to be considered for risk identification?	a. Pre-Mortem b. Prompt List c. FMEA d. Root Cause Identification	
39.	Which of the following statements is true regarding Risk, Variance and Standard Deviation?	a. Risk increases as Standard Deviation and Variance increase b. Risk decreases as Standard Deviation and Variance increase c. Risk decreases as Standard Deviation decreases and Variance increases d. Risk increases as Standard Deviation decreases and Variance increases	
40.	You just identified a new external risk during the executing phase that may impact your project positively. What is your first step?	a. Develop a Risk Response and assign a Risk Owner b. Update the Risk Breakdown Structure c. Perform Qualitative Risk Analysis d. Perform Quantitative Risk Analysis	
41.	You are managing a complex project that introduces deliverables and processes new to the organization. There are a number of ambiguities that need to be addressed as potential risks. Which estimating method will serve this project best?	a. Analogous b. Bottom Up c. Parametric d. Expert	
42.	Which of the following statements is true regarding the Perform Quantitative Risk Analysis process?	a. Identifies risks with the greatest impact on project objectives and takes time. b. It is a fast and objective analysis methodology. c. It is only accomplished only as required and provides a prioritized list of risks. d. Uses numerical analysis and scores risks by probability and impact.	

43.	Your team wants to analyze threats and opportunities to identify both negative and positive risks. Which tool is best suited for this objective?	a. Delphi Technique b. SWOT Analysis c. Nominal Group Technique d. Root Cause Analysis	
44.	You have been tasked to complete a Risk Management Plan as soon as possible to support your project. Which tool and technique will not be required at this time?	a. Planning Meetings b. Expert Judgment c. Analytical Techniques d. Enterprise Environmental Factors	
45.	You are trying to determine who has responsibility to develop Risk Response Plans and monitor status. You optimally assign this to the:	a. Project Manager b. Sponsor c. Risk Owner d. Risk Activity Manager	
46.	A team member wants to know the definition of a Trigger. What should you tell her?	a. The probability that a risk will occur b. Any risk that has not yet been identified c. Any risk event with potential impact d. Any event that predicts a risk will occur	
47.	Risk Governance policy and procedure is applied during which Project Risk Management process?	a. Control Risks b. Identify Risks c. Plan Risk Responses d. Plan Risk Management	
48.	What type of analysis will allow you to predict the potential impact of multiple risks on key project schedule and cost objectives?	a. Qualitative Risk Analysis b. Subjective Risk Analysis c. Risk Breakdown Structure Analysis d. Quantitative Risk Analysis	
49.	You are asked to use a weighted estimation method given a pessimistic estimate of 33 days, most likely estimate of 25 days, and optimistic estimate of 11 days. What should you estimate for the duration?	a. 24 Days b. 23 Days c. 25 Days d. 33 Days	

50.	Decision Tree Analysis looks at scenarios and recommends selection of the option:	a. With the highest success probability b. With the lowest failure probability c. With the highest EMV d. With the lowest EMV	
51.	Which statement regarding Lessons Learned is most correct?	a. They are best conducted at the closure of the project. b. They aid in refining risk policies and practices. c. They are always conducted formally to assist future Project Managers. d. They address past and future situations that will likely impact future projects.	
52.	You completed a risk response activity and are left to act upon part of the risk impact that the response did not address. How do you refer to the remaining risk?	a. Residual Risk b. Secondary Risk c. Emergent Risk d. Risk Trigger	
53.	Your Risk Governance rules require you to strive for contracts that reduce cost and schedule risk to the buyer. Which contract type should you try to avoid?	a. Fixed Price with Incentives b. Time and Material c. Cost Plus Percentage of Costs d. Cost Plus Award Fee	
54.	You determine that excessive rain could delay your project by weeks. You determine to deal with the event if it occurs but develop a Contingency Plan to satisfy stakeholders. Which risk response did you use?	a. Mitigation b. Avoidance c. Transference d. Acceptance	
55.	A tool that shows the impact of multiple factors on a single variable is called:	a. Triangular Distribution b. Tornado Diagram c. Uniform Distribution d. PERT	

56.	Which statement is true regarding the Perform Quantitative Analysis process?	a. It must be performed to analyze all risks. b. It always occurs prior to the Perform Qualitative Analysis process. c. Requires the Stakeholder Register as a key input. d. May not be performed on every project.	
57.	You are given three estimates to complete a key project activity. The pessimistic estimate is 25 days. Most likely is 16 days and the optimistic estimate is 10 days. How much time should you plan for the activity?	a. 15 Days b. 16 Days c. 17 Days d. 19 Days	
58.	The primary benefit to consider ISO as part of your Risk Governance policy is?	a. Provides standard Risk Breakdown Structures for use in all project types. b. Provides best practices and standards to improve risk. management performance c. Provides inspections of projects to score risk management effectiveness. d. Describes standard risk tolerance ratings for various project priorities.	
59.	You found some key deficiencies in the Project Management Plan as a result of a Risk Review. You need to generate formal change requests for additional Contingency Reserves. Which project Risk Management process did you perform?	a. Plan Risk Management b. Identify Risks c. Plan Risk Responses d. Control Risks	
60.	You reviewed the WBS and an activity must be completed that your team may not have the expertise to accomplish. You find another team who is willing to take on the work and do the job. What risk response did you use?	a. Mitigation b. Transference c. Avoidance d. Acceptance	

61.	Project Managers must understand and balance all of the following constraints except:	a. Risk b. Communications c. Customer Satisfaction d. Quality	
62.	You are in the process of reviewing Work Performance Reports to determine overall risk management effectiveness. Which process are you performing?	a. Perform Qualitative Risk Analysis b. Perform Quantitative Risk Analysis c. Control Risks d. Plan Risk Responses	
63.	You identified new risks and updated the probability of two risks on the Watch List. What action did you complete?	a. Risk Reassessment b. Risk Audit c. Variance Analysis d. Technical performance Measurement	
64.	There is an opportunity to improve return on investment from your project by 20% from potential supplier discounts. You will need to order more supplies to achieve the discount. You found another Project Manager who needs the same supplies. Which risk response should you choose?	a. Enhance b. Share c. Exploit d. Mitigate	
65.	Which of the following Project Risk Management processes does not occur in the Project Planning Process Group?	a. Plan Risk Management b. Control Risks c. Perform Qualitative Risk Analysis d. Identify Risks	
66.	Your team is debating which risk responses are most appropriate for opportunities. Which responses fit this categorization?	a. Mitigate, Enhance, Accept b. Avoid, Exploit, Share c. Accept, Transfer, Exploit d. Exploit, Enhance, Accept	
67.	A Project Manager was reviewing a Stakeholder Register as part of her risk management duties. During which Process Group is the Stakeholder Register developed?	a. Initiating b. Planning c. Executing d. Monitoring and Controlling	

68.	You want to use a Group Creativity Technique that enhances Brainstorming and uses a voting process to rank order ideas. Which Technique will work best?	a. Root Cause Analysis b. Sensitivity Analysis c. Delphi Technique d. Nominal Group Technique	
69.	You are identifying risks and want to consider risks at both the micro and macro levels. Which input will allow you to identify and track risks at a summary, control account, or work package level?	a. Risk Management Plan b. Published Checklists c. Work Breakdown Structure d. Scope Statement	
70.	A Project Manager is analyzing the potential effects of product failures to determine potential project risks. Which is the most appropriate tool and technique to use for this purpose?	a. Ishikawa Diagram b. Flow Chart c. SWOT d. FMEA	
71.	Molly is reviewing the return potential for proposed projects. She knows that there is a guarantee of a $50,000 return if she selects Project A. Based on risk, there is a 20% possibility of an additional $30,000 return as well. Molly should list total returns potential as?	a. $50,000 b. $80,000 c. $20,000 d. $56,000	
72.	A Project Manager identified a number of new risks that developed due to misconceptions and erroneous information received during the project planning stage. What was probably not accomplished at the appropriate level?	a. Assumptions Analysis during Identify Risks b. Assumptions Analysis during Qualitative Risk Analysis c. Risk Data Quality Assessment during Identify Risks d. Risk Data Quality Assessment during Qualitative Risk Analysis	
73.	Which process ensures risk policies and procedures are understood, followed, applied, and effective?	a. Risk Management b. Risk Governance c. Configuration Management d. Organizational Process Assets	

74.	You were surprised by a risk event that was not recorded on your Risk Register. The first thing you should do is to implement a:	a. Contingent Response Strategy b. Fallback Plan c. Workaround d. Emergency Task Plan	
75.	You are looking for a response that will reduce the probability of exceeding allocated budget on a project activity. Which type of response is best?	a. Mitigate b. Enhance c. Avoid d. Exploit	
76.	You are developing Contingency Plans to respond to risk when a Trigger is identified. This type of strategy is referred to as a :	a. Strategies for Positive Risks or Opportunities b. Risk Urgency Assessment c. Fallback Plan d. Contingent Response Strategy	
77.	You have an opportunity to expedite project schedules if you spend an additional $25,000 to ensure a potential risk cause occurs. What response should you use?	a. Exploit b. Mitigate c. Transfer d. Enhance	
78.	A Risk Team member who is tasked to specifically implement risk responses is referred to as a:	a. Risk Action Owner b. Project Manager c. Risk Response Specialist d. Risk Owner	
79.	You identified a risk that will result from a Contingency Plan to generate a contract with a secondary parts supplier. How do you refer to this risk?	a. Residual Risk b. Secondary Risk c. Emergent Risk d. Risk Trigger	
80.	A Project Manager is sharing a copy of the Cost Management Plan with her team. Which Project Risk Management process is the Project Manager preparing to perform?	a. Identify Risks b. Control Risks c. Plan Risk Responses d. Plan Risk Management	

81.	Sarah is seeking input to help perform a risk identification activity for a critical IT project. Which Information Gathering Techniques should she consider?	a. Sensitivity Analysis, Delphi Technique, and Brainstorming b. Delphi Technique, Brainstorming, and Interviewing c. Sensitivity Analysis, Delphi Technique, and Interviewing d. Sensitivity Analysis, Brainstorming, and Interviewing	
82.	Which of the following activities update the Risk Register?	a. Identify Risks, Perform Qualitative Risk Analysis, Plan Risk Responses b. Perform Quantitative Risk Analysis, Plan Risk Responses, Control Risks c. Perform Quantitative Risk Analysis, Plan Risk Responses, Identify Risks d. Perform Qualitative Risk Analysis, Identify Risks, Perform Quantitative Risk Analysis	
83.	The cost of a project is $32,000. There is a 40% chance of returns of $25,000 and a 60% chance of returns of $60,000. What is the potential value of this project?	a. $14,000 b. $53,000 c. $46,000 d. $28,000	
84.	Which is the greatest source for potential conflict you may encounter in a project?	a. Budget b. Personalities c. Leadership Styles d. Schedules	
85.	Which statement regarding risk management is true?	a. Risk probability has a tendency to increase as the project progresses. b. Most risks are identified during the Project Executing phase. c. Risk of not completing a project successfully is highest at the beginning of the project. d. Quantitative Risk Analysis is mandatory for all projects.	

86.	A Project Manager discovered that certain Probability and Impact Risk Ratings were biased. What action should be taken initially by the Project Manager?	a. Report the issue to the Sponsor and request assistance to ensure the situation does not occur again. b. Update the Risk Management Plan to ensure risk thresholds are clearly defined. c. Take action to correct the biased Risk Ratings to better reflect the true analysis of the risks. d. Create a bias to reflect the initial results by weighting higher priority risks.	
87.	You are asked to provide input on the level of detail specific risk responses should contain. What is the best advice you can provide?	a. All responses should provide a high-level overview of the required response. b. Responses should provide an appropriate level of detail to implement Contingency Plans. c. Level of detail must be validated by the Project Manager and sponsorship team. d. Risk response details should vary based on the overall priority of the risk itself.	
88.	A Project Manager just completed an extensive review to measure the effectiveness of the overall Risk Management Process. What activity did he perform?	a. Risk Audit b. Risk Reassessment c. Risk Response d. Risk Review	
89.	Technical Performance Measurement is a key function of the Control Risks process. What is the best source to use this tool and technique?	a. Risk Management Plan b. Quality Management Plan c. Scope Baseline d. Risk Register	
90.	A Project Manager is attempting to define the risk tolerance of key stakeholders. Which of the following is a risk tolerance category?	a. Communications b. Conflict c. Customer Satisfaction d. Adoption	

91.	Nicole is using an estimation technique that uses estimates from prior projects similar to hers. What estimating technique is she using?	a. Parametric b. Analogous c. Three Point d. Bottom Up	
92.	Consistent risk assessment, risk management, and risk communication are primary goals of the:	a. PMO b. Project Manager c. Sponsor d. Risk Governance Body	
93.	A Project Manager is developing a Probability and Impact Matrix and wants to ensure that the risk-rating rules are tailored to the project. What is the best source to find specific guidance on risk-rating rules?	a. Enterprise Environmental Factors b. Organizational Process Assets c. Earned Value Reports d. Quality Management Plan	
94.	The cost of a potential option to complete a key activity is $90,000. If this option is adopted, there is a 70% chance of returns of $120,000. There is a 30% chance of returns of $140,000. What is the Expected Monetary Value of this option?	a. $170,000 b. $50,000 c. $36,000 d. $40,000	
95.	Project assumptions are a major source of potential risks. Which document defines key assumptions impacting a project?	a. Risk Breakdown Structure b. Communications Management Plan c. Scope Statement d. Stakeholder Register	
96.	You want to identify key customers to ensure they are interviewed and participate in the Risk Management Process. Which input will provide you with this information?	a. Stakeholder Register b. Stakeholder Management Strategy c. Communications Management Plan d. Lessons Learned	
97.	A number of risk-related contractual decisions were identified as pertinent to a project. These decisions were likely developed as a result of:	a. Plan Risk Management b. Perform Quantitative Risk Analysis c. Plan Risk Responses d. Control Risks	

98.	Which goal is not associated with the Control Risks process?	a. Perform Sensitivity Analysis activities b. Implement Risk Responses as needed c. Monitor Residual and Secondary Risks d. Monitor Risk Trigger conditions	
99.	You are performing a Checklist Analysis to identify potential risks. Which fact is true regarding Checklist Analysis?	a. Provides an in-depth analysis of project risks b. Analysis is time consuming but well worth the time investment c. Technique is not used to provide an initial high level analysis d. Checklists are generally developed based on Lessons Learned	
100.	You are not confident that you have solid probability and cost impact data for each risk. Based on this assessment, which technique should not be used?	a. Qualitative Risk Analysis b. Expected Monetary Value Analysis c. Risk Categorization d. Risk Data Quality Assessment	
101.	You identified a risk that requires you to add non-project time between two activities to mitigate. What is this non-project time referred to as?	a. Lag b. Lead c. Buffer d. Break	
102.	You are looking at a normal distribution with a mean of 20. The Standard Deviation is 2. Within what range can you expect results to occur approximately 68% of the time?	a. 18 to 22 b. 16 to 24 c. 14 to 26 d. 8 to 32	
103.	The Schedule Management Plan is a key input required to effectively complete:	a. Plan Risk Responses and Identify Risks b. Plan Risk Responses and Control Risks c. Perform Quantitative Risk Analysis and Control Risks d. Identify Risks and Perform Quantitative Risk Analysis	

104.	A Risk Data Quality Assessment is a tool and technique used in which risk management process?	a. Plan Risk Management b. Perform Qualitative Risk Analysis c. Perform Quantitative Risk Analysis d. Control Risks	
105.	A Project Manager wants to develop a contract that poses the least amount of Cost Risk to the buyer. Which contract best suits this purpose?	a. Firm Fixed Price b. Time and Material c. Cost Plus Percentage of Cost d. Request for Quote	
106.	A project has a budget at completion of $60,000. As of today, it is 40% complete. This is better than the 30% planned completion level forecast for this point in the project. A total of $25,000 has been expended for the project. Which statement is true?	a. Project is behind schedule b. Project is ahead on budget c. Schedule Variance is negative d. Cost Variance is negative	
107.	Using the information in question 106, what is the project's current SPI?	a. .96 b. 1.33 c. -$1,000 d. $6,000	
108.	A Project Manager is concerned that the stakeholder's scoring of probability and impact was affected by erroneous perceptions of project goals. What does this situation represent?	a. Risk Utility b. Motivational Bias c. Conceptual Bias d. Cognitive Bias	
109.	The Project Risk Score for the ABC project is higher than acceptable by stakeholders. What risk metric is excessive?	a. Risk Rating b. Risk Exposure c. Risk Probability d. Risk Impact	
110.	The Risk Management Plan is a key input for all of the following activities except:	a. Identify Risks b. Plan Risk Management c. Perform Quantitative Risk Analysis d. Plan Risk Responses	

111.	An unexpected risk occurred that will impact the project's Schedule and Cost Performance Baselines. What is your best response to this circumstance?	a. Develop a workaround to deal with this occurrence. b. Perform variance and trend analysis to ensure the risk does not occur again. c. Initiate an immediate Risk Audit to respond. d. Determine levels of reserve analysis to transfer the risk.	
112.	Gilmere is developing strategies to deal with threats to her project. What process is Gilmere performing?	a. Plan Risk Responses b. Risk Management Planning c. Control Risks d. Quality Assurance	
113.	Patti's Sponsor stated he will accept a budget variation of + or – 5%. This is an example of a:	a. Management Reserve b. Control Threshold c. Risk Tolerance d. Heuristic	
114.	You encounter a risk that could allow you to reduce time to complete a key project activity by two weeks. You want to take action to respond to this risk. Which risk responses are most appropriate?	a. Acceptance or Mitigation b. Mitigation or Exploitation c. Exploitation or Enhancement d. Enhancement or Acceptance	
115.	What is the most likely result of communications blockers?	a. Schedule delays b. Conflict c. Cost overruns d. Information delays	
116.	There are hygiene factors and motivating agents. Hygiene factors such as salary, working conditions, benefits, etc. can only destroy motivation. They do not increase motivation. Motivating factors such as responsibility, growth, and achievement are those that increase motivation. Who is responsible for this theory?	a. Maslow b. McClelland c. McGregor d. Hertzberg	

117.	The process of refining risk practices and policies by using Lessons Learned is a key task that falls under:	a. Risk Communication b. Risk Analysis c. Risk Response Planning d. Risk Governance	
118.	You just completed a Risk Data Quality Assessment and determined three risks require additional information prior to determining their overall priority. Which process step did you perform?	a. Perform Qualitative Risk Analysis b. Plan Risk Management c. Perform Quantitative Risk Analysis d. Plan Risk Reponses	
119.	You developed an enhance response to a risk on the Risk Register. The risk occurred and you are now implementing the Contingency Plan. What is the term used to define this event?	a. Issue b. Problem c. Benefit d. Residual Risk	
120.	A stakeholder manages using what is best described as a hands-off style. Which leadership type best describes this manager?	a. Facilitative b. Consultative c. Participative d. Laissez-Faire	
121.	A risk event occurred and a risk response was implemented. You scheduled a Risk Audit. Which Project Management Process Group are you performing?	a. Planning b. Executing c. Monitoring and Controlling d. Closing	
122.	You completed a Brainstorming session with key stakeholders. You did not attain the information you required. What action may have impacted the effectiveness of this session?	a. Evaluated all ideas b. Used sticky notes c. Requested experts to attend d. Took time to log all inputs	
123.	You are using a Supporting Leadership Style to manage your team. Which stages of team development is best suited to this leadership style?	a. Forming and Storming b. Norming and Performing c. Forming and Norming d. Performing and Storming	

124.	You have new information that needs to be documented on the project Risk Register. Which Project Risk Management processes require Risk Register updates?	a. Plan Risk Management and Identify Risks b. Identify Risks and Perform Qualitative Risk Analysis c. Perform Qualitative Risk Analysis and Plan Risk Management d. Plan Risk Responses and Control Risks	
125.	You need critical input from experts to plan a controversial IT project. You plan to use a tool and technique which reduces fear of reprisal. You will consolidate all inputs and provide a final report to all who contribute. Which tool and technique are you using?	a. Nominal Group Technique b. Interviews c. Sensitivity Analysis d. Delphi Technique	
126.	You are currently analyzing risks to determine their probability and impact scores. What risk management process are you performing and where do you find definitions for probability and impact?	a. Perform Qualitative Risk Analysis/Risk Register b. Perform Quantitative Risk Analysis/Risk Register c. Perform Qualitative Risk Analysis/Risk Management Plan d. Perform Quantitative Risk Analysis/Risk Management Plan	
127.	Which of the following entries would most likely not be part of a Risk Management Plan?	a. Risk categories b. Link to resource Breakdown Structure c. Reporting formats d. Risk Scores for urgent risks	

128.	You identified four risks as follows. How much in contingency reserves should you request? • Risk A: 20% chance ($20,000) • Risk B: 50% chance $10,000 • Risk C: 40% chance $40,000 • Risk D: 10% chance ($100,000)	a. ($7,000) b. $7,000 c. $70,000 d. ($100,000)	
129.	Fran just completed a Risk Audit. What project activity did she perform?	a. Update and publish the Risk Register b. Document results from the quantitative risk analysis process c. Close out a risk no longer a threat d. Review a risk response that occurred	
130.	A Project Manager developed a tool that shows risk causes and preventative controls, along with consequences and controls to mitigate impact if the risk occurs. What tool did the Project Manager develop?	a. Risk Management Plan b. Bowtie Analysis c. Tornado Diagram d. Ishikawa Diagram	
131.	A Project Manager is using What If scenarios to calculate potential results. She believes use of this modeling technique will help determine which risks have the greatest impact on a project. What tool is being used?	a. Sensitivity Analysis b. FMEA c. Delphi Technique d. Nominal Group Technique	

132.	Ben plans to use a tool to consolidate ideas through individual Brainstorming sessions into a single map to reflect commonality and differences in understanding, and to generate new ideas. What is this tool?	a. Ishikawa Diagram b. Pareto Chart c. Idea/Mind Mapping d. Affinity Diagram	
133.	You are reviewing desired commitment levels for key stakeholders and determine strategies to gain buy-in for risk related activities are not yielding results. You determine to adjust the current strategies in an effort to gain the support you need. What process are you performing?	a. Identify Stakeholders b. Control Stakeholder Engagement c. Manage Stakeholder Engagement d. Plan Stakeholder Management	
134.	A project team plans to use the Monte Carlo tool as a means to determine the probability of meeting certain project time and cost goals. What tool and technique does Monte Carlo support?	a. Critical Chain Method b. Crashing c. Simulation d. Resource Smoothing	
135.	A new risk was identified that may impact your project negatively. Which statement is true regarding this situation?	a. Most appropriate responses include mitigate, accept, and exploit b. Document risk in the Risk Register and begin Quantitative Risk Analysis c. Place risk on the Watch List and determine further actions during Risk Reassessment d. Perform Qualitative Risk Analysis and calculate Risk Score	

136.	A new Risk Owner provided a probability rating of five on a five point scale. You are skeptical about this rating, and are not confident the new Risk Owner used valid data. Which tool and technique will help the Project Manager validate the input?	a. Risk Probability and Impact Assessment b. Probability and Impact Matrix c. Risk Data Quality Assessment d. Risk Urgency Assessment	
137.	During the Perform Quantitative Risk Analysis process, a team defined accelerators that can move a project toward a successful conclusion, and resistors that can move a project toward an unsuccessful conclusion. What tool and technique did they use?	a. Decision Trees b. Force Field Analysis c. Fault trees d. Logic Diagrams	
138.	You are reviewing industry studies of similar projects by risk specialists, and risk databases from industry or proprietary sources to better qualify risks. How would this input be best classified?	a. Organizational Process Assets b. Enterprise Environmental Factors c. Risk Breakdown Structure d. Risk Probability and Impact Assessment	
139.	Betty is performing Qualitative Risk Analysis and using a tool that shows how the top 20% of all causes result in 80% of the effects. She plans to use this data to determine risk probabilities. Which tool is she using?	a. Ishikawa Diagrams b. SWOT Analysis c. Risk Breakdown Structure Analysis d. Pareto Charts	
140.	Which of the following tasks is not a primary goal of stakeholder engagement?	a. Assess stakeholder risk tolerance b. Develop processes for risk assessment c. Prioritize project risk d. Promote risk ownership	

141.	Which statement is true regarding the Perform Quantitative Risk Analysis process?	a. Predicts likely outcomes b. Always performed c. Subjective d. Prioritizes individual risks	
142.	Risk Register updates may occur as a result of all processes except:	a. Plan Risk Management b. Perform Qualitative Risk Analysis c. Perform Quantitative Risk Analysis d. Plan Risk Responses	
143.	Paul's manager is not willing to accept a straight 10% risk contingency. He stated that the current project Paul is managing has negative and positive risks that offset one another. In addition, Paul's manager is confident that the worst or best case cost or time scenarios, and the probability of each risk occurring can be quantified. Which risk analysis and modeling technique should Paul consider?	a. Sensitivity Analysis b. Expected Monetary Value c. Decision Tree Analysis d. Monte Carlo Technique	
144.	A key stakeholder has a negative attitude regarding risk management and its value. Where would you document this situation and develop a strategy to try to influence the stakeholder's attitude in a positive direction?	a. Stakeholder Register b. Risk Register c. Stakeholder Management Plan d. Risk Management Plan	
145.	An approach to problem solving, learning, or discovery that employs a practical method not guaranteed to be optimal or perfect, but sufficient for the immediate goals is referred to as:	a. Heuristics b. Nominal Technique c. Minimal Analysis d. Sensitivity Analysis	

146.	Which skills should a Project Manager use to best promote a common understanding of the value of risk management?	a. General Management b. Risk Management c. Stakeholder Management d. Interpersonal	
147.	A Project Manager is looking for guidance on how to categorize Risk Scores. She can't decide whether to classify the risk as urgent, or move the risk to the Watch List. Which tool and technique should she review for guidance?	a. Risk Data Quality Assessment b. Organizational Process Assets c. Contingent Response Strategies d. Probability and Impact Matrix	
148.	Which of the following tools would not be considered as a Group Creativity Technique?	a. Brainstorming b. Monte Carlo Technique c. Nominal Group Technique d. Delphi Technique	
149.	Paul identified a number of risks that may result in either positive or negative returns. He plans to use a type of sensitivity analysis that uses a bar chart to show potential risk scenarios and their impact. What tool will Paul use?	a. Residual Risk Analysis b. Risk Reassessment c. Tornado Diagram d. Interrelationship Digraph	
150.	You completed the Identify Risk process but feel strongly that all possible risks were not identified. You want to select the best tool and technique to revisit risk identification to determine if there are additional risks. Which tool and technique will serve you best?	a. Interviews b. Cause and Effect Diagrams c. Affinity Diagrams d. Prompt Lists	

Final Test Solutions and Explanations

Question #	Response	Rationale
1.	D	Qualitative risk analysis is subjective. This eliminates options A and C. Option B is incorrect. Assessing the probability of achieving specific project objectives is quantitative. Option D using a Probability and Impact Matrix is qualitative.
2.	C	Management Reserves are reserves for unknown unknowns or unknown risks. Contingency Reserves are for known risks. Options B and D are not types of reserves.
3.	D	Remember to follow the input-tool and technique-output method of performing activities. Options A and B are outputs in the Risk Management Plan. Option C is the tool and technique after you have the inputs. Option A is a key input. Gather inputs first.
4.	D	The initial Risk Register lists risk, cause, initial Risk Owners, categories, and responses. Option D satisfies these criteria. All other activities occur in later steps of the Risk Management Process.
5.	C	Risk C has the highest priority, based on its overall Risk Score of 16. Risk A scores 10, Risk B scores 12, and Risk D scores 10.
6.	A	Option A is true regarding the Perform Qualitative Risk Analysis process. Qualitative Risk Analysis addresses individual risks. All other options are true for the Perform Quantitative Risk Analysis process.
7.	C	A Project Manager spends approximately 90% of his or her time communicating.
8.	A	Analytical tools key focus areas include business, tools, and people factors.

9.	B	Expect some Expected Monetary Value (EMV) questions on the certification exam. To calculate Contingency Reserve requirements, multiply the probability times the impact for each risk and sum the total. Keep in mind that there are positive and negative risks. In this scenario, total Contingency Reserve requirement is: • Risk A: 40% probability with $8,000 impact = -$3,200 • Risk B: 20% probability with $5,000 impact = -$1,000 • Risk C: 10% probability with ($10,000 impact) = ($1,000) • Risk D: 80% probability with $6,000 impact = -$4,800 Total = $8,000 • We need $8,000 added to our project for contingency funds. • Risks A, B, and D are negative risks. Risk C is a positive risk.
10.	C	Risk B occurred. We used $5,000 from our Contingency Reserves. This leaves us with $8,000 - $5,000 = $3,000 left.
11.	B	The team described is most likely in the norming stage. A supporting leadership style is best suited to this team. Coaching is best when the team is forming. Facilitative is best during storming. Autocratic leadership is best when a decision must be made quickly.
12.	A	Option A is correct. Option B is wrong. You need to gain buy-in—it's not automatic. Option C is incorrect. You need to prioritize risks and manage the top risks. Otherwise you'll burn out your team. Option D is not correct as well. Don't anticipate risk tolerances—know them.
13.	A	There are four key project objectives. They include scope, time, cost, and quality. Communications is not a project objective. It is a knowledge area that supports achievement of objectives.
14.	B	Option B is the best answer. Option A is partially correct. Risks can also impact a project positively. Option C is not correct. Risk is not always an unknown. However, it is always uncertain. Option D is not totally correct. Risks can occur during all Process Groups.

15.	B	90% is a popular number. A good risk management program can reduce problems by that much!
16.	D	A Look Up Table is synonymous with a Probability and Impact Matrix. This is an Organizational Process Asset. The Look Up Table is documented in the Risk Management Plan.
17.	C	Your overall processes and strategy to support risk management are documented in the Risk Management Plan.
18.	A	Remember the PIER-C acronym? You identified risks and listed newly found risks, or Emergent Risks in the Risk Register. The next step is evaluation. The first evaluation method to employ is Qualitative Risk Analysis.
19.	B	Categorization of risks normally leads to improved and more focused risk responses. This is the best answer.
20.	A	Always add newly identified risks to the Risk Register. You can evaluate and develop responses after they are listed.
21.	C	A Matrix organizational model uses resources from across the organization. It seems as if you work for two bosses. A Projectized organization consists solely of Project Managers doing project work. A Functional, or Silo, organization uses resources from strictly within the organization.
22.	D	The probability of a risk occurring in the second month is the same as in subsequent months unless something has changed. The scenario did not mention any changes.
23.	B	Communications channels are calculated as $((n*(n-1))/2$. In this case, the solution is $(8*7)/2 = 28$.
24.	C	Standard Deviation is calculated as (Pessimistic – Optimistic)/6. The solution is $(18-6)/6 = 2$.
25.	A	The Integrated Change Control component ensures all changes are reviewed from a risk standpoint. Configuration Management looks only at the functional and physical characteristics of the project's product.
26.	C	The Communications Management Plan defines which stakeholders require specific information. It defines the communications activity, preferred media, frequencies, and impacted stakeholders.

27.	A	The beta distribution shows results or events that peak on either side of the mean. A uniform distribution would show an equal probability of any event to occur as depicted on the graph. A triangular distribution shows results peaking at the mean and falling off rapidly as you move from the mean. The normal distribution represents the typical Bell Curve.
28.	D	Option A is a good answer. Many Risk Owners are assigned from the team. However, the team is not the only source from which to find Risk Owners. Past Project Managers may or may not be candidates for Risk Owners. Sponsors could be Risk Owners, but that is a low probability scenario. The best answer is Option D. A Risk Owner can be any stakeholder.
29.	B	Add all low probability and low impact risks to the Watch List. The other options are not applicable to the question.
30.	C	You need to understand the contents of the Risk Management Plan. Change management is not a category defined in the Risk Management Plan. Therefore, Options A, B, and D are incorrect.
31.	A	The Quality Management Plan is an output of Plan Quality that defines applicable standards for a project. It is an input to the Identify Risks process step.
32.	C	Option C is correct. Using questionnaires to solicit input from experts match the Delphi Technique approach. Root Cause Analysis uses Cause and Effect Analysis tools to find the root cause of a specific problem. Sensitivity analysis is What If using variations of inputs. Nominal Group Technique breaks groups into smaller groups to control Brainstorming, prevent domination by an individual, and rank orders inputs.
33.	D	A Risk Breakdown Structure breaks risks into categories. It then identifies specific risks to consider in each category.
34.	B	Risk Utility is a term used to describe stakeholder's willingness to accept risk. Risk averse means stakeholders have a low tolerance for risk. A risk threshold is a numeric indicator of tolerance levels. Risk bias is a measure of how attitudes and/or perceptions can alter Risk Ratings.

35.	C	Risk Metalanguage is a definition that describes the best practice for developing a risk statement. The three components are Cause, Risk, and Effect. Options B, C, and D do not state the three criteria.
36.	A	Application of all tools and techniques take time. However, interviews normally take the most time to complete. Interviews require time to discuss risk with each expert individually.
37.	D	Path convergence occurs when multiple activities flow into or out of a single activity. The Project Network Diagram shows activity dependencies and how all activities interrelate.
38.	B	A Prompt List is nothing more than a list of potential risk categories to consider for project risk identification.
39.	A	Risk increases as Standard Deviation increases. Standard Deviation and Variance have a positive correlation. As one increases, the other increases and vice versa.
40.	C	Always start the Perform Qualitative Risk Analysis process when a new risk is identified. Determine the probability, impact, and calculate a Risk Score. You would add this risk to the Risk Register. However, this was not an available response, so you choose the best answer.
41.	B	Bottom Up Estimating is best when a project type is new, or there are ambiguities that must be addressed. Parametric is a math model that depends on accurate unit and impact data. Analogous, also known as Top Down or Expert, is best for recurring projects where there are few ambiguities.
42.	A	There is only one option that is 100% correct. Make sure you read all answers before responding. It is not a fast method, which rules out Option B. It does not provide a list of prioritized risks. That occurs during Qualitative Risk Analysis. This makes C an incorrect response. Option D is also incorrect. Scoring risks by probability × impact is a function of Qualitative Risk Analysis.
43.	B	SWOT analysis is a tool and technique that allows you to determine strengths that may lead to opportunities and weaknesses that may lead to threats.

44.	D	The three tools and techniques associated with the Plan Risk Management process are Analytical Techniques, Expert Judgement, and Meetings. Enterprise Environmental factors are an input, not a tool and technique.
45.	C	The Project Manager assigns Risk Owners to all risks. The Risk Owner is responsible for developing responses, monitoring status, and leading the response effort. Note the optimal reference. If a Risk Owner is not assigned, the Project Manager becomes the default Risk Owner.
46.	D	A Trigger is an event that precedes a risk. For example, clouds and thunder would be a Trigger that lets you know rain is on its way.
47.	A	The Control Risks process of Project Risk Management is when governance activities are conducted.
48.	D	Quantitative Risk Analysis looks at multiple risks and assesses their cumulative impact on satisfying schedule and cost objectives.
49.	A	The only weighted estimation method you need to remember is PERT. In this case, you apply the formula of (O +4ML +P)/6 = Estimate. When you do the math, you end up with 144/6 which equals 24 Days.
50.	C	Decision Tree Analysis looks at multiple scenarios and tries to determine the option that provides the best overall Expected Monetary Value (EMV).
51.	B	Lessons Learned should be accomplished at the end of each project phase. Lessons Learned may be conducted formally or informally, and document only those events that have occurred or are now occurring. They allow for updates of risk policy and practices.
52.	A	Residual Risks are risks that remain after a risk response is implemented. It is best to develop Contingency Plans for Residual Risks and highlight them on Risk Registers.
53.	C	The Cost Plus Percentage of Cost contract is the one that poses the greatest Cost Risk to a buyer. Note that the Fixed Price Contract places the Cost Risk on the seller.
54.	D	Determining to deal with an event if it occurs is an acceptance response strategy. In this scenario, you are applying *active acceptance*. This is development of a Contingency Plan to deal with a risk if it occurs.

55.	B	A Tornado Diagram shows the impact of multiple factors on a single variable. Note that Tornado Diagrams are the result of applying the Sensitivity Analysis tool and technique.
56.	D	The Quantitative Risk Analysis process is not always performed. The decision to use the Perform Quantitative Risk Analysis process depends on project priority, benefits of performing the analysis, etc.
57.	C	Always use Three Point averaging unless you are directed to use PERT or a weighted estimation method. To solve this problem, add the 3 estimates given together and divide them by three to calculate the average. (25+16+10 = 51/3 = 17)
58.	B	ISO is an organization that shares standards and best practices that may apply to your project. It is a governance tool.
59.	D	Remember the inputs, tools and techniques, and outputs of all Risk Management Process activities. Change Requests are only generated as an output of Control Risks.
60.	B	Transference is a risk response strategy that transfers work or accountability to a third party. This scenario defines a transfer action.
61.	B	Remember the Seven Constraints model? This includes time, cost, scope, customer satisfaction, resources, risk, and quality. Communications is an important knowledge area but not a constraint.
62.	C	Work Performance Reports are a key input required to perform the Control Risks process.
63.	A	Risk Reassessment is the action of identifying new risks and reassessing current risks on the Risk Register. This technique is performed during Control Risks.
64.	B	The share response enlists the support of a third party to participate and share in an opportunity. In this scenario, the opportunity is a 20% ROI increase. You are sharing the opportunity with the other Project Manager who will benefit from the discount.
65.	B	All Risk Management Process activities occur in planning with one exception. Control Risks occurs in the Monitoring and Controlling Process Group.
66.	D	There are four strategies to respond to positive risks or opportunities. They include exploit, share, enhance, and accept.

67.	A	The Stakeholder Register is an input to the Identify Risks process. It is developed during the project initiating phase.
68.	D	Option D provides a "by the book" definition of Nominal Group Technique. This is a great method to use when identifying and evaluating risks.
69.	C	The Work Breakdown Structure breaks activities out to a summary, control account, or work package level. This key input to the Identify Risks process satisfies the scenario best.
70.	D	Failure Modes and Effect Analysis (FMEA) is a tool that identifies potential failure modes and determines the effects of each failure. Understand acronyms for the test. Not all acronyms are spelled out!
71.	D	This is a Decision Tree question that calculates Return + Return. We have a fixed return of $50, 000 PLUS a Risk Adjusted Return using Expected Value of (20% × $30,000). Add the two together and we end up with $50,000 + $6,000 = $56,000.
72.	A	Assumptions Analysis occurs during the Identify Risks process. This analysis reviews information believed to be true and verifies the information as either true or false.
73.	B	This question provides the exact definition of Risk Governance. Remember the definition.
74.	C	A workaround is the first action you take when you need to respond to an unknown risk that catches you by surprise. It is accomplished during Control Risks.
75.	A	Mitigation is a response strategy that reduces either the probability or impact of a negative risk event.
76.	D	Risk responses initiated when a Trigger event occurs are referred to as Contingent Response Strategies.
77.	A	Exploit is a response strategy implemented in an attempt to make a risk cause or event to occur. It is used for positive risks or opportunities.
78.	A	A Risk Action Owner is assigned by a Risk Owner. Their specific job is to implement Contingency Plans.
79.	B	Secondary Risks are risks that result as a direct result of a planned risk response. Secondary Risks should always be listed in the Risk Register and should never have a higher priority than the primary response they are linked to.

80.	A	Here is another case of emphasizing the importance of knowing the inputs, tools and techniques, and outputs of all Risk Management Process activities. The Cost Management Plan can be an input for either the Identify Risks process or the Perform Quantitative Risk Analysis process.
81.	B	Delphi Technique, Brainstorming, and Interviewing are three Information Gathering Techniques used as tools of the Identify Risks process. Note that Delphi Technique is also listed as a Group Creativity Technique in the *PMBOK* as well.
82.	B	The Risk Register is created during the Identify Risks process. Therefore, options A, C, and D were not correct. The Risk Register is updated during the processes of Perform Qualitative Risk Analysis, Perform Quantitative Risk Analysis, Plan Risk Responses, and Control Risks.
83.	A	This is an Expected Monetary Value question. To solve, add up the EMV values which represent returns and subtract the cost. The result is the value of the project. Doing the math: $.4 \times \$25,000 = \$10,000$ $.6 \times \$60,000 = \underline{\$36,000}$ Total: $\quad \$46,000 - \$32,000 = \$14,000$
84.	D	Schedules are the number one cited source of potential conflict.
85.	C	The only correct statement is Option C. The risk of not completing a project successfully is highest at the beginning of a project.
86.	C	Biased Risk Ratings will occasionally occur. The priority is to adjust the Risk Rating as soon as possible to eliminate bias and reflect accurate analysis of probability and impact.
87.	D	The detail of risk responses is based on the overall priority of the risk itself. Not all risks require equal levels of detail.
88.	A	The correct response is a Risk Audit. Risk Reassessment is a reassessment of individual risks. A Risk Review looks at potential risk responses to ensure they are still appropriate. Risk responses are accomplished when a risk occurs.

89.	B	Technical Performance Measurement determines if actual performance matches planned performance. Targets, metrics, etc. are used to perform this tool and technique. This information is documented in the Quality Management Plan.
90.	C	Risk tolerance categories reflect the Seven Constraints model. Measures risk, customer satisfaction, resources, scope, cost, time, and quality tolerance levels.
91.	B	Analogous uses information from similar past projects for estimating. Analogous is also referred to as Expert or Top Down Estimating.
92.	D	Consistent risk assessment, risk management, and risk communication are primary goals of the Risk Governance Body.
93.	B	According to the *PMBOK*, risk-rating rules for an organization are generally specified in Organizational Process Assets.
94.	C	You are investing $90,000. There is a 70% chance of returns of $120,000. Using EMV, this equates to (70% × $120,000) = $84,000. There is a 30% chance of returns of $140,000. Using EMV, this equates to (30% × $140,000) = $42,000. Add the EMV values ($84,000 + $42,000) = $126,000. Subtract the investment of $90,000. The result is a value of $36,000.
95.	C	Assumptions can be found in the Project Scope Statement.
96.	A	The Stakeholder Register provides key information on all project stakeholders including customers.
97.	C	Risk related contractual decisions may result from the Plan Risk Responses process when transfer or share strategies are determined as required.
98.	A	Sensitivity Analysis is a tool and technique of Quantitative Risk Analysis. Options B through D reflect objectives of the Control Risks process.
99.	D	Checklists are generally developed based on Lessons Learned. It is a fast process that provides an initial high level analysis of risks. It does not provide an in-depth review.
100.	B	Options A, C, and D are all associated with Qualitative Risk Analysis which, is always performed. Expected Monetary Value analysis depends on solid probability and dollar/schedule impact data. You do not have this data. Therefore, you cannot use Expected Monetary Value analysis.

101.	C	A buffer is non-project time that is added between two activities to mitigate risk. This is normally a function of the Critical Chain method of scheduling.
102.	A	Results occur approximately 68% of the time within 1 Sigma of the mean. To determine the range at 1 Sigma, subtract the Standard Deviation from the mean to determine the low end estimate. This is $20 - 2 = 18$. Add the Standard Deviation to the mean to determine the high end estimate. This is $20 + 2 = 22$. A range of 16 to 24 would reflect 2 Sigma. A range of 14 to 26 reflects 3 Sigma, etc.
103.	D	The Cost Management Plan and Schedule Management Plan are inputs in both processes of Identify Risks and Perform Quantitative Risk Analysis.
104.	B	The Risk Data Quality Assessment is a tool and technique used during the Perform Qualitative Risk Analysis process.
105.	A	The Fixed Price family of contracts puts the Cost Risk on the seller. Cost Reimbursement and Time and Material type contracts put the Cost Risk on the buyer.
106.	D	You may be presented with an Earned Value Technique question. This type of question is typical. • BAC is $60,000. • Since the project is 40% complete, your Earned Value (EV) is (40% × $60,000) = $24,000. • You had planned to be 30% complete at this point in the project, Planned Value (PV) is (30% × $60,000) = $18,000. • Your Actual Costs (AC) is $25,000. Option A is not correct. The project is not behind schedule. Calculate Schedule Variance as (EV-PV). The result is +$6,000. The project is ahead of schedule. Option B is also not correct. The project is not ahead on budget. Calculate Cost Variance as (EV-AC). The result is -$1,000. The project is behind on budget. Option C is incorrect. The Schedule Variance (SV) is positive. Option D is the answer. The Cost Variance (CV) is indeed negative.

107.	B	The Schedule Performance Index (SPI) is calculated by EV/PV. Options C and D are the Cost Variance and Schedule Variance results. Option A is the Cost Performance Index (EV/AC). Option B is correct. The SPI is ($24,000/$18,000) = 1.33.
108.	D	Cognitive bias occurs when individual stakeholder perceptions impact Risk Ratings. Risk Utility is a measure of overall stakeholder risk tolerance. Motivational bias occurs when stakeholders intentionally bias Risk Ratings to satisfy ulterior motives. Conceptual bias is not a recognized form of bias in the *PMBOK*.
109.	B	The Risk Exposure of a project is the sum of all individual Risk Scores. Risk Ratings are assigned to probability and impact estimates for individual risks. Multiply Risk Ratings for probability and impact to achieve an individual Risk Score.
110.	B	The Risk Management Plan is a key output of the Plan Risk Management process. It is an input for all other Project Risk Management activities.
111.	A	A workaround is defined as the response to an unplanned risk. Keep the project moving is always a first priority.
112.	A	Risk Response Planning is the process that requires you to develop strategies for positive risks (opportunities) and/or negative risks (threats).
113.	B	Risk tolerance is a broad statement of acceptable risk. A control threshold defines the acceptable level of variation in numeric terms such as dollars, percentages, time, etc.
114.	C	The risk of saving time is a positive risk. This eliminates Options A and B. Mitigation is a negative risk response. The scenario indicates you want to act on this risk. This eliminates Acceptance as an option presented in Option D. Enhancement and Exploitation are both viable responses to a positive risk.
115.	B	Communications blockers or noise factors most likely result in conflict. The Project Manager must mitigate these blockers.
116.	D	Hertzberg is responsible for the motivational theory that deals with hygiene factors and motivating agents.
117.	D	The process of refining risk practices and policies by using Lessons Learned is a key task that falls under the Risk Governance domain.

118.	A	The Risk Data Quality Assessment is a tool and technique used when you are in the Perform Qualitative Risk Analysis process.
119.	C	A positive risk that occurs is called a Benefit. This is the opposite of a negative risk that occurs which is called an issue.
120.	D	Laissez-Faire is a leadership style that is best explained as hands-off. All other styles listed in the responses involve of interaction.
121.	C	A Risk Audit occurs during the Control Risks process. This activity occurs in the Monitoring and Controlling Process Group.
122.	A	Do not evaluate ideas during Brainstorming. The goal of Brainstorming is to solicit ideas you will evaluate later.
123.	B	The Supporting Leadership Style is best used during the Norming and Performing stages of the Tuckman Model for team development.
124.	D	Risk Register updates occur during the processes of Perform Qualitative Risk Analysis, Perform Quantitative Risk Analysis, Plan Risk Responses, and Control Risks.
125.	D	Delphi Technique helps you attain expert input and mitigates stakeholder fears.
126.	C	Analyzing risks to determine their Probability and Impact Scores occurs in the Perform Qualitative Risk Analysis process. Definitions for probability and impact are included in the Risk Management Plan.
127.	D	Risk Scores for all risks are not calculated until the Perform Qualitative Risk Analysis process. However, definitions for probability and impact are included.
128.	B	You have two negative risks valued at 50% × $10,000 = $5,000 and 40% × $40,000 = $16,000. Total negative risks are $21,000. You have two positive risks valued at 20% × ($20,000) = ($4,000) and 10% × ($100,000) = ($10,000). Total positive risks are valued at ($14,000). You ask for the difference, which is $7,000.
129.	D	A Risk Audit is a review of a response to a risk that occurred. It answers the question, "How did we do?"
130.	B	Bowtie Analysis is a tool that shows risk causes and preventative controls, along with consequences and controls to mitigate impact if the risk occurs.

131.	A	Sensitivity Analysis uses several What If scenarios to calculate potential results. Sensitivity Analysis is a modeling technique that helps determine which risks have the greatest impact on a project.
132.	C	A tool to consolidate ideas through individual Brainstorming sessions into a single map to reflect commonality and differences in understanding, and to generate new ideas is the definition of an Idea/Mind Map.
133.	B	Review Project Stakeholder Management. The Control Stakeholder Engagement is where you review strategies and adjust as required.
134.	C	Monte Carlo is a tool that is applied when using Simulation.
135.	D	You should document the new risk in the Risk Register. Next step is the Perform Qualitative Risk Analysis process. Calculate probability × impact to determine a Risk Score. Option D is the only 100% correct answer.
136.	C	The purpose of a Risk Data Quality Assessment is to determine the validity of data used to evaluate risks.
137.	B	Force Field Analysis defines accelerators that can move a project toward a successful conclusion, and resistors that can move a project toward an unsuccessful conclusion. Let's put this in the context of risk management. Accelerators correlate well to opportunities. Resistors correlate well with threats.
138.	B	Industry studies of similar projects by risk specialists, and risk databases from industry or proprietary sources to better qualify risks are categorized as Enterprise Environmental Factors.
139.	D	Pareto Prioritization Analysis shows the top 20% of problems which are normally responsible for 80% of the issues. Remember the 20/80 metric and always associate this with Pareto Charts.
140.	B	Develop policies, processes, and procedures for risk assessment is a goal of Risk Strategy and Planning. All other options are activities related to stakeholder engagement.
141.	A	Quantitative Risk Analysis predicts likely outcomes. Qualitative Risk Analysis addresses individual risks, is subjective, is always accomplished, and evaluates using probability × impact.

142.	A	The Risk Register is created during the Identify Risks process. It is updated during the processes of Perform Qualitative Risk Analysis, Perform Quantitative Risk Analysis, Plan Risk Responses, and Control Risks.
143.	B	Probability × best/worst case time or cost scenario is Expected Monetary Value. Sensitivity analysis (Option A) and Monte Carlo (Option D) use What If scenarios to determine a potential range of results. Decision tree analysis looks at multiple scenarios and quantifies cost and/or returns from each using weighted criteria.
144.	C	The Stakeholder Management Plan defines current and desired states for key stakeholders and a strategy to align the current and desired states.
145.	A	An approach to problem solving, learning, or discovery that employs a practical method not guaranteed to be optimal or perfect, but sufficient for the immediate goals is referred to as Heuristics.
146.	D	The best way to promote a common understanding of the value of risk management is through the use of interpersonal skills.
147.	D	The Probability and Impact Matrix breaks out risks by priority and importance. The relative urgency of this risk can be compared to others to determine its placement.
148.	B	Group Creativity Techniques include Brainstorming, Delphi Technique, Nominal Group Technique, Idea/Mind Mapping, and Affinity Diagramming.
149.	C	A Tornado Diagram is a type of sensitivity analysis that uses a bar chart to show potential risk scenarios and their impact.
150.	C	Affinity diagramming is the best method to use when it is believed that all possible risks were not identified.

APPENDIX C: Acronyms

Acronym	Long Title
AC	Actual Costs
AHP	Analytical Hierarchy Process
BAC	Budget at Completion
CPI	Cost Performance Index
CV	Cost Variance
EMV	Expected Monetary Value
ETC	Estimate to Completion
EV	Earned Value
FFP	Firm Fixed Price Contract
FMEA	Fault Modes and Effect Analysis
FP	Fixed Price Contract
IRGC	International Risk Governance Council
ISO	International Organization for Standardization
NPV	Net Present Value
OSHA	Occupational Safety and Health Administration
PDCA	Plan, Do, Check, Act
PERT	Program Evaluation Review Technique
PIER-C	Plan, Identify, Evaluate, Respond, Control
PMBOK	*Project Management Body of Knowledge*
PMI	Project Management Institute
PMO	Project Management Office
PMP	Project Management Professional
PV	Planned Value
RACI	Responsible, Accountable, Consult, Inform
RBS	Risk Breakdown Structure
RMP	Risk Management Professional
SD	Standard Deviation
SME	Subject Matter Expert
SPI	Schedule Performance Index
SV	Schedule Variance
SWOT	Strengths, Weaknesses, Opportunities, Threats
WBS	Work Breakdown Structure
WPD	Work Performance Data
WPI	Work Performance Information
WPR	Work Performance Report

APPENDIX D: Glossary of Terms and Index

Term	Chapter	Definition
1 Sigma	5	Standard Deviation level on a Bell Curve. Results occur approximately 68.26% of the time.
2 Sigma	5	Standard Deviation level on a Bell Curve. Results occur approximately 95.46% of the time.
3 Sigma	5	Standard Deviation level on a Bell Curve. Results occur approximately 99.73% of the time.
6 Sigma	5	Standard Deviation level on a Bell Curve. Results occur approximately 99.99985% of the time.
Acceptance (Accept)	6	Response to either a negative or positive risk. No action is prescribed, should the risk occur.
Achievement Motivation Theory	9	Motivational model developed by David McClelland. States people are motivated by some combination of achievement, affiliation, and empowerment.
Active Acceptance	6	You develop contingency plans to address the risk when it occurs. This may be a necessary step to when it is necessary to increase stakeholder confidence that you have an approach for risks you accepted.
Activity Cost Estimates	3	Output of Estimate Costs. Provides cost estimates for the project.
Activity Duration Estimates	3	Output of Estimate Activity Durations. Provides time durations for the project.
Adjourning	9	Fifth step in the Tuckman Model. Project is complete and team disbands.
Affinity Diagramming	3	Method uses the intellectual power of a group to place risks into categories. This is the best method to use if you believe you have not identified all possible risks.

Term	Chapter	Definition
Analogous Estimating	9	An estimating method where time and cost estimates are provided by an expert source. Also referred to as Top Down or Expert Estimating.
Analytical Hierarchy Process	5	Provides a comprehensive, hierarchical and rational framework for structuring a decision problem, for representing and quantifying its elements, for relating those elements to overall goals, and for evaluating alternative solutions.
Analytical Techniques	2	A tool and technique used in the Plan Risk Management process. Reviews people, tools, and business factors impacting the Risk Management Plan.
Assumption	1, 2	Information we believe to be true but have not yet validated. Assumptions are always risks until validated.
Assumptions and Constraint Analysis	2, 3	Action of validating or dismissing an assumption through analysis and research. Ensuring constraints are identified and analyzed and impact is documented.
Autocratic	9	Make decisions without input from others.
Avoidance (Avoid)	6	The focus of this risk response strategy is to eliminate a negative cause of the risk. Try to take action to ensure the risk does not occur. This is often accomplished by removing people and/or activities.
Benefit	1	Term that depicts a positive risk or opportunity that occurred.
Beta Distribution	5	Probability peaks on either side of the mean.
Bias	4	Any event or attitude that can skew a Probability or Impact Risk Rating.
Bottom Up Estimating	9	A form of estimating that aggregates individual work package in puts from the people who are performing the project work.

Term	Chapter	Definition
Bowtie Analysis	5	Risk evaluation method that can be used to analyze and demonstrate causal relationships in high risk scenarios. The method takes its name from the shape of the diagram that you create.
Brainstorming	3	Open forum where members generate ideas and solve problems. A facilitator logs input. Brainstorming is one method used for attaining expert input.
Buffer	5, 9	Non-working time you add between two activities to account for identified risks. For example you lay concrete, wait two days for the concrete to set, and then begin construction. The buffer is the two day wait.
Buffer Analysis	9	Analysis to determine if buffers are required.
Business Risk	1	These risks can either be opportunities or threats. They can cause either profit or loss.
Categorization	4	Grouping of risks and based on common causes. Allows for development of better responses.
Cause and Effect Diagrams	3	Graphic depictions of risk causes and potential effects on the project. Also called Ishikawa Diagrams, Root Cause Identification, or Fishbone Diagrams.
Change Control Log	9	Tool used to document and manage project change requests.
Checklist Analysis	3	Quick and simple approach which can be used for an initial high-level analysis of risks. Checklist analysis will identify new risks that are not on the checklist. This is a limitation.
Closing Process Group	9	The fifth Process Group in the PMI framework. Goal is to close out projects, contracts, and transition deliverables.
Coaching	9	Train and instruct others on how to perform the work. Sharing talents, skills, competencies etc. with others.

Term	Chapter	Definition
Cognitive Bias	4	Bias based on perceptions. The perception becomes a reality that influences the Risk Rating.
Communications Blockers (Noise)	9	Anything that can interfere with the communications model. Leads to conflict.
Communications Channels	9	The number of potential conversations that can occur within a project team.
Communications Management Plan	9	Output from Plan Communications. Defines interactions among stakeholders. Shows who is available to share risk information.
Communications Model	9	Model that shows flow of communication between a sender and receiver, and shares challenges to overcome and communications objectives to achieve.
Compliance	2	Ensure key organizational policy and procedure is adhered to. Accommodate key governance criteria and methods.
Configuration Management	9	Part of Integrated Change Control. Process used to manage changes to the project's functional and physical characteristics.
Conflict Management	9	Handle, control, and guide to achieve resolution.
Consensus Building	9	Solve problems based on group input. Strive for decision buy in agreement.
Consequence	4	*See* Impact.
Constraints	2	Anything that can limit the team's options. Boundaries that must be acknowledged and addressed. The seven-sided constraint provides categories of constraints to consider. Also includes standards, regulations, and Enterprise Environmental Factors.

Term	Chapter	Definition
Consultative	9	Invite others to provide input and ideas.
Contingency Plan	6, 7	Your primary response plan to address a risk.
Contingency Reserves	1, 2, 7	Extra time or budget added to the project to account for known risks. Also referred to as reserves for known unknowns.
Contingent Response Strategy	6	A risk response strategy that calls for implementation of a contingency plan when a Trigger indicates the risk is about to occur.
Control Risks	1	The sixth process in the PMI risk framework. Goal is perform periodic Risk Reassessments, Respond to Risks as required, and report status.
Control Stakeholder Engagement	9	Fourth step in Project Stakeholder Management. Goal is to update the Stakeholder Management Plan.
Cost Management Plan	3, 5	Defines how risk budgets and contingency/management reserves will be reported and accessed.
Cost Reimbursement Contract	8	A buyer proposes work and contracts the seller's expertise. Total costs are not known until the end of the contract. Cost risk is on the buyer.
Crashing	6	This is a compression technique where you use resources from one activity and apply them to another. This is a common form of enhancement or mitigation.
Critical Chain Method	9	Time Management method of determining if buffers are required.
Cultural and Social Environment	9	Understanding of how projects can affect people, and how people affect the project.

Term	Chapter	Definition
Data Gathering and Representation Techniques	5	Tool and technique of the Perform Quantitative Risk Analysis process. Includes Interviewing, Probability Distributions, and Three Point Estimating.
Decision Making	9	Apply right style to ensure effective decisions are made in a timely manner.
Decision Tree Analysis	5	Describes a scenario under consideration and uses available data to determine the most economic approach. The primary objective is to determine which scenarios provide the best overall EMV.
Delphi Technique	3	Gain inputs and consensus through anonymous inputs. Reduces fear of reprisal. Delphi Technique is also a method used to attain expert input. Surveys and questionnaires are popular methods.
Diagramming Techniques	3	Tool and Technique used during the Identify Risks process. Includes Cause and Effect Diagrams, Flowcharts, and Influence Diagrams.
Directive	9	Tell people what to do.
Documentation Reviews	3	Tool and technique used during the Identify Risks process. Goal is to identify potential risks from project documentation.
Earned Value Technique	8	PMI's preferred method of performance reporting. Analyzes Planned Value, Actual Costs, and Earned Value to determine schedule and budget performance.
Effect	4	*See* Impact.
Effective Communications	9	Understand communications channels, informational requirements, and be effective
Emergent Risk	1	Risk that was not identified during the initial Identify Risk process step. Risk is discovered after the project begins.

Term	Chapter	Definition
Enhancement (Enhance)	6	This risk response aims to increase the probability of the risk occurring or the impact of a risk if it occurs.
Enterprise Environmental Factors	2, 3, 4, 5	Risk attitudes and tolerances. The degree of risk an organization is willing to tolerate. Also includes culture, systems, and values that support an organization.
Executing Process Group	9	The third Process Group in the PMI framework. Goal is to implement the Project Management Plan.
Expectancy Theory	9	Employees believe effort leads to performance. Performance should be rewarded based on their expectations. Rewards promote further productivity.
Expected Monetary Value (EMV)	5	Method used to establish contingency reserve requirements for both budget and schedule. EMV is quantified by multiplying probability × the best or worst case cost/time scenario.
Expert Estimating	9	*See* Analogous.
Expert Judgement	2, 3, 4, 5, 6	Common tool and technique supporting multiple risk processes. Indicates that a Project Manager needs to find the expertise they need to plan effectively. Project management is a team sport.
Exploitation (Exploit)	6	This is a risk response where you take action to make cause occur. You work to make the risk happen. It may require additional time or resources to use the exploit response method.
Facilitative	9	Coordinate and solicit the input of others. A good Project Manager is facilitative.
Failure Modes and Effect Analysis (FMEA)	3	Tool that identifies potential failure modes, determines effects of each failure, and seeks ways mitigate the probability and impact of each failure.
Fallback Plan	6	A plan you will implement if your primary risk response contingency plan fails. A secondary plan.

Term	Chapter	Definition
Fishbone Diagram	4	*See* Cause and Effect Diagrams.
Fixed Price Contract	8	A Fixed Price contract is a price provided by a seller to complete a contract. Cost Risk is on the seller.
Force Field Analysis	5	Defines accelerators that can move a project toward a successful conclusion, and resistors that can move a project toward an unsuccessful conclusion.
Forming	9	First step in the Tuckman Model. Team comes together for first time. Leader strategy is to tell.
Functional Manager	9	Key stakeholder. Individual who manages or controls the personnel assets you need to implement a project.
Functional Organization	9	Organizational structure where communications and power flow from top to bottom. Often referred to as a Silo organization.
Futures Thinking	5	Analyzes scenarios by opening perspectives beyond immediate constraints. Futures Thinking enhances the capacity of policy-makers and practitioners to anticipate change, grasp opportunities, and cope with threats.
Goldplaters	7	Groups or individuals that try to add additional functionality without using the formal change management process. They are the primary perpetuators of scope creep.
Governance	8	The process of ensuring risk policies and procedures are understood, followed, consistently applied, and effective.
Group Creativity Techniques	3	Tool and Technique used during the Identify Risks process. Includes Brainstorming, Delphi Technique, Nominal Group Technique, Affinity Diagramming, and Idea/Mind Mapping.
Hertzberg's Theory	9	There are hygiene factors and motivating agents. Hygiene factors as can only destroy motivation. Motivating factors are those that increase motivation.

Term	Chapter	Definition
Heuristics	4	Any approach to problem solving, learning, or discovery that employs a practical method not guaranteed to be optimal or perfect. Sometimes referred to as Rules of Thumb.
Human Resource Management Plan	3	Plan created in during the Plan Human Resource Management process. Identifies project organizational chart and roles and responsibilities and includes Staffing Management Plan.
Identify Risks	1, 3	The second process in the PMI risk framework. Goal is to develop an initial Risk Register.
Identify Stakeholders	9	First step in Project Stakeholder Management. Goal is to develop a Stakeholder Register.
Impact	2, 4	A qualification of the consequences to the project if a risk event occurs.
Influence Diagrams	3	Method includes graphical representations of situations showing causal influences, time ordering of events, and other relationships between variables and outcomes.
Influencing	9	Share power; get others to cooperate toward common goals.
Information Gathering Techniques	3	Methods for gathering information. Includes Brainstorming, Delphi Technique, Interviews, Root Cause Identification, and Nominal Group Technique.
Initiating Process Group	9	The first Process Group in the PMI framework. Goals are to develop a Project Charter and Stakeholder Register.
Insurable Risk	1	These are also called Pure risks. These risks are always negative or threats. In addition, they are outside the Project Manager's control. Examples are natural disasters, fire, theft etc.
Integrated Change Control	9	Process established to manage changes to a Project Management Plan. Process is normally included as part of the project Communications Management Plan.

Term	Chapter	Definition
Integration	1	Risk management must be integrated with all project management activities to be successful. It is not an isolated event.
International and Political Environment	9	Applicable laws and current political climates you must deal with on a project.
International Organization for Standardization (ISO)	8	This organization develops standards based on best practices and encourages their use by all who subscribe to ISO methodology.
International Risk Governance Council (IRGC)	8	This organization's primary goal is to facilitate understanding and manage risks that impact society, human health, safety, and the environment as a whole.
Interview	3, 4, 5	One-on-one meetings with key stakeholders or experts in a given field. A drawback of this technique is that it takes time and is slow.
Ishikawa Diagram	4	*See* Cause and Effect Diagrams.
Issue	1	Term that depicts a negative risk or threat that occurred.
Iterative	1	Any activity or process that is repeated. The risk management process is very iterative.
ITO	1	PMI approach to defining processes. Begin with *Inputs*, use *Tools and Techniques* to transform inputs into *Outputs*.
Known Risks	1, 7	Risks identified during the Project Risk Management process and documented on the Risk Register.

Term	Chapter	Definition
Known Unknowns	7	*Same as Known Risks.*
Leadership	9	Focus efforts of the group toward a common goal. Get things done through others.
Leading	9	Level of Commitment designator. Stakeholder is supportive and actively engaged in the project.
Lessons Learned	2, 3, 4, 5, 7, 8, 9	Formal or informal Lessons Learned from past projects. Lessons learned should be documented and shared in an effort to improve the effectiveness of Project Managers on future projects.
Likelihood	4	*See* Probability.
Lognormal	5	Values on a Bell Curve that are skewed; not symmetric like a normal distribution during Monte Carlo Simulation.
Lookup Table	2, 4	*See* Probability and Impact Matrix.
Manage Stakeholder Engagement	9	Third step in Project Stakeholder Management. Goal is to implement the Stakeholder Management Plan.
Management Reserves	1, 2, 7	Extra time or budget added to the project to account for unknown risks. Also referred to as reserves for unknown unknowns.
Maslow's Hierarchy of Needs Theory	9	Maslow stated that motivation occurs in a hierarchal manner. Physiological – Safety – Social – Esteem – Self Actualization needs must be satisfied in this order.
Matrix Organization	9	Hybrid organization where there are some Functional and some Projectized elements.

Term	Chapter	Definition
McGregor's Theory X and Y	9	Theory X managers believe people are not to be trusted and must be watched. Theory Y managers believe people want to achieve and can be self–directed.
Mitigation (Mitigate)	6	Risk response that takes actions to reduce the probability of the risk occurring, or the impact of risk if it occurs. This could be thought of as developing a Plan B.
Monitoring and Controlling Process Group	9	The fourth Process Group in the PMI framework. Goal is to ensure adherence to the Project Management Plan.
Monte Carlo	1, 5	Form of What If Scenario Analysis and uses optimistic, most likely and pessimistic estimates to determine the probability of meeting cost and/or schedule objectives.
Most Likely	5	The average scenario when estimating time or cost factors. Term used in Three Point Estimation.
Motivation	9	Create environment to meet project objectives and offer self-satisfaction.
Motivational Bias	4	Occurs when stakeholders intentionally try to bias ratings one way or another.
Negative Risk	1, 3	Any risk event that may result in a threat to project objectives.
Negotiation	9	Confer with concerned parties to make agreements acceptable to all.
Net Present Value (NPV)	5	A measure of financial value for a project that considers the time value of money. Generally, the highest NPV value depicts the optimal project to select.
Neutral	9	Level of Commitment designator. Stakeholder has yet to determine level of support.

Term	Chapter	Definition
Nominal Group Technique	3	Technique similar to Brainstorming. You collect input from a select group, analyze inputs, and rank order the results.
Normal Distribution	5	Normal distribution is also referred to as the Bell Curve. A normal distribution model uses averages and Sigma intervals to show the potential range of values over the length of a Bell Curve.
Norming	9	Third step in the Tuckman Model. Team overcomes individual focus and issues and now begins to focus on project work. Leader strategy is to participate.
Objectives	1, 9	Measureable goals a project aims to accomplish. They include scope, time, cost, and quality.
Optimistic	5	The best case scenario when estimating time or cost factors. Term used in Three Point estimation.
Organizational Process Assets	2, 3, 4, 5, 7	Includes risk categories, definitions, templates, roles and responsibilities, information on organizational risk tolerances etc.
Parametric Estimating	9	An objective estimating method that uses defined cost, time and unit data.
Pareto Prioritization Analysis	4	Pareto Charts track problems or issues from most to least. The idea is that 20% of all causes result in 80% of all effects.
Passive Acceptance	6	This type of acceptance occurs when no contingency plans are created to address the risk.
Path Convergence	4	Defined as multiple activities flowing into or from a central activity. Increases risk.
PDCA	1	Acronym stands for Plan, Do, Check, Act. Methodology adapted for the PMI Project Management Framework to follow.

Term	Chapter	Definition
Perform Qualitative Risk Analysis	1, 2, 4	The third process in the PMI risk framework. Goal is to qualify all risks using probability × impact to calculate a Risk Score.
Perform Quantitative Risk Analysis	1, 5	The fourth process in the PMI risk framework. Goal is to update the Risk Register using mathematical and other quantitative methods and determine probable outcomes.
Performing	9	Fourth step in the Tuckman Model. Team is now self-organized and highly effective. Leader strategy is to delegate.
PERT	5	A form of Three Point Estimation that uses a weighted method to calculate the best estimate based on Pessimistic, Most Likely, and Optimistic estimates.
Pessimistic	5	The worst case scenario when estimating time or cost factors. Term used in Three Point Estimation.
Physical Environment	9	Understanding how the project will affect, or is affected, by the surrounding physical environment.
PIER-C	1, 2, 3, 4, 5, 6, 7	Acronym developed by Daniel Yeomans to show the end-to-end risk management methodology. Stands for Plan, Identify, Evaluate, respond, and Control.
Plan Risk Management	1	The first process in the PMI risk framework. Goal is to develop a Risk Management Plan.
Plan Risk Responses	1	The fifth process in the PMI risk framework. Goal is to develop a response to risks, as required.
Plan Stakeholder Management	9	Second step in Project Stakeholder Management. Goal is to develop a Stakeholder Management Plan.
Planning Meetings and Analysis	2	The key tool and technique used to develop a Risk Management Plan during the Plan Risk Management process.

Term	Chapter	Definition
Planning Process Group	9	The second Process Group in the PMI framework. Goal is to develop a Project Management Plan.
Political and Cultural Awareness	9	Use politics and power skillfully to achieve project objectives.
Positive Risk	1, 3	Any risk event that may result in an opportunity to project objectives.
Pre-Mortem	3	Method used to identify potential risks before a project begins. Compare your project to past projects that were similar. Try to determine what could go right or wrong with your project before the project begins.
Probability	2, 4	Potential for a risk to occur. Scoring systems include percentages, a numeric scale (1-5 for example), etc.
Probability and Impact Matrix	2, 4	Matrix that shows ratings and overall priority determinations. The Risk Matrix you use can be simple or elaborate depending upon the prioritization methodology you select. Also called a lookup table. Documented in Risk Management Plan.
Probability Distributions	5	Estimates the potential of a risk event to occur over a pre-described range. You need to be familiar with a number of distribution types.
Process Flow Chart	3	Reveal how systems function, interrelate, and serve as a superb means of identifying potential risks.
Process Related Criteria	2	Required processes that must be followed to ensure project success.
Procurement Documents	3	Includes key documentation from Project Procurement Management. May include agreements, contracts, Statements of Work, etc.
Project Charter	2	Creation and approval of a Project Charter authorizes resources for risk planning. It also defines the scope of the project at a high level and is used to ensure project planning supports the initial project objectives.

Term	Chapter	Definition
Project Documents	3	Includes assumption log, Work Performance Reports, Earned Value Technique metrics, network diagrams, baselines etc.
Project Management Office (PMO)	1	Organization that may share risk policies and procedures, best practices, ensure Risk Governance, etc.
Project Management Plan	2	The approved and accepted plan that constitutes the Project Baseline. All risk planning is part of the overall Project Management plan.
Project Related Criteria	2	Required project results for cost, time, and scope.
Project Risk	1	An uncertain event or condition that, if it occurs, has a positive or negative effect on at least one of the project's objectives.
Project Risk Score	1, 4	This score reflects the uncertainty of the project as a whole by adding the total of all individual Risk Scores.
Project Schedule Network Diagram	4, 9	Output of Sequence Activities. Shows dependencies for all activities and where paths converge.
Project Scope Statement	9	Key output of Define Scope. Defines range of possibilities for project and deliverables.
Projectized Organization	9	Organizational structure where focus is on projects. Many PMOs are Projectized.
Prompt List	3	Generic list of categories where risks may be found. Used to prompt ideas and risk identification.
Pure Risk	1	*See* Insurable Risk.
Qualitative Risk Analysis	4	Subjective risk evaluation process where risks are scored and prioritized by probability × impact. Process is always performed.

Term	Chapter	Definition
Quality Management Plan	3, 9	Defines specific approach to quality to include metrics, targets, standards, checklist for Quality Control, process improvement opportunities etc.
Quantitative Risk Analysis	5	Objective risk evaluation process that numerically analyzes the impact of multiple risks to the project. Helps determine probability that stated budgetary and schedule outcomes can be met.
Quantitative Risk Analysis and Modeling Techniques	5	Tool and technique of the Perform Quantitative Risk Analysis process. Includes multiple mathematical and other modeling techniques.
RACI	9	Method of designating specific Roles and Responsibilities to project stakeholders. Designate as Responsible, Accountable, Consult, Inform, or a combination of one or all.
Regression Analysis	5	A statistical process for estimating the relationships among variables. There are multiple types of Regression Analysis.
Reserve Analysis	7	Process of reviewing management and contingency reserves to ensure they support project needs.
Reserves	2, 7	Extra time or budget added to the project to account for risks. Effective risk management provides a basis for identifying and requesting reserves.
Residual Risk	6, 7	Risks that remain after a response is implemented. For example, a response may address 80% of the risk impact. The remaining 20% is the Residual Risk.
Resistant	9	Level of Commitment designator. Stakeholder does not support the project.
Resource Breakdown Structure	2, 3, 4, 9	Key output of the Estimate Activity Resources process. This output shows what resources are required for the project. This is a key document used during risk identification.
Risk Action Owner	6	This individual is assigned by a Risk Owner to help implement approved risk responses.

Term	Chapter	Definition
Risk Adverse	2	Indicates stakeholder unwillingness to accept risk.
Risk Attitude	1, 2	How stakeholders perceive the significance and priority of risks and overall project risk management.
Risk Audit	7	Audits that examine responses to risk and answer the question, "How did we do?" Risk audits also measure of the overall effectiveness of the risk management process.
Risk Based Critical Chain Analysis	5	Defined as the use of buffers to mitigate potential high risk network diagram configurations.
Risk Breakdown Structure (RBS)	2	Lists risk categories and sub-categories in hierarchical order to help identify risks. Places risks in categories, and defines specific risks applicable to the type of project being managed in that category.
Risk Breakdown Structure Analysis	4	Tool and technique used in the Perform Qualitative Risk Analysis process to determine potential probability of risk by reviewing the Risk Breakdown Structure.
Risk Data Quality Assessment	4	Tool to determine if Probability and Impact Scores are accurate and unbiased. You may determine that the data you used is not sufficient. If this is the case, you need to annotate the risk as requiring further information to improve understanding.
Risk Exposure	1	Term that defines the level of risk on a project. The Project Risk Score determines risk exposure. Acceptable levels of risk exposure are based on stakeholder attitudes, tolerances, and thresholds.
Risk Management Department	1	Entity within an organization tasked to address risk management as their primary job function.
Risk Management Plan	2, 3, 4, 5, 6, 7	Plan created during the Plan Risk Management process that describes how the entire end-to-end risk management process will work.
Risk Management Process	1	A six-step approach designed to help you manage end-to-end project risk.

Term	Chapter	Definition
Risk Metalanguage	3	A best practice for writing risk statements. Uses a cause-event-impact methodology.
Risk Metric Trend Analysis	4	The practice of trending Risk Scores throughout a project to determine if risk management activities are having positive results.
Risk Owner	3, 6	Stakeholders assigned to manage risks. They develop responses, monitor risk status, and implement contingency and fallback plans if required. Risk Owners can be any stakeholder in the project.
Risk Probability and Impact Assessment	4	Tool and technique used in the Perform Qualitative Risk Analysis process. Gives each risk a Probability and Impact Rating, which are multiplied to calculate a Risk Score.
Risk Rating	4	A score that reflects the probability or impact of an individual risk.
Risk Rating Within Project	4	Method of prioritizing risks by Risk Score.
Risk Reassessment	7	Control Risks activity that identifies new risks and requires reassessment of existing risks. Ensures outdated risks are closed. Also ensures new risks are identified when changes to the project are made.
Risk Register	3, 4, 5, 6, 7, 9	Output created during the Identify Risks process. Includes risk definition, owner, causes, initial responses, and categorization.
Risk Response Plan	6	*See* Contingency Plan.
Risk Review	7	Review to analyze potential risk responses to see if they are still appropriate. Part of risk reassessment. May include changing order or priority of risks, adjusting severity of risks, or monitoring Residual Risks.
Risk Score	4	A score that reflects the uncertainty of an individual risk by multiplying the Probability Risk Rating by the Impact Risk Rating.

Term	Chapter	Definition
Risk Threshold	1, 2	An objective statement of risk tolerance. For example, stakeholders are willing to accept up to 5% cost overruns.
Risk Tolerance	1, 2	A statement of how much risk a stakeholder is willing to tolerate. Generally stem from risk attitudes.
Risk Urgency Assessment	4	Analysis of all risks to determine their relative priority based on Probability and Impact Risk Ratings.
Risk Utility	2	Describes a person or organization's willingness to accept risk.
Risk Metalanguage	3	Method to effectively identify and describe risks. The three-step method to develop a risk statement is to define the Cause, Risk, and Effect of the risk.
Root Cause Analysis	4	*See* Cause and Effect Diagrams.
Root Cause Identification	4	*See* Cause and Effect Diagrams.
Scenario Planning	5	Looks at potential scenarios that may impact a project and determines risk factors for each scenario.
Schedule Baseline	9	The primary output of project time management. This is the approved and accepted project schedule. The baseline may be adjusted through the project's formal Integrated Change Control process to account for risk.
Schedule Management Plan	3, 5	Output from Develop Project Management Plan. Defines how schedule contingencies will be reported and accessed.
Scope Baseline	3, 4, 9	Includes Scope Statement, WBS, and WBS Dictionary. Scope Statement lists assumptions.

Term	Chapter	Definition
Scope Creep	7, 9	Changes to the project's scope that are not processed through the formal change control process.
Scope Statement	9	*See* Project Scope Statement.
Scrum of Scrums	9	Meetings held where ScrumMasters from each team periodically meet to discuss issues and concerns among the teams.
Secondary Risk	6, 7	A risk that results from a risk response. For example, a response to use a vendor to perform project work could lead to potential vendor management risks.
Sensitivity Analysis	5	Modeling technique that helps determine which risks have the greatest impact on the project. Also referred to as What If Scenario Analysis.
Seven Constraint Model	1	Model that drives risk tolerance levels. Includes scope, time, cost, quality, risk, customer satisfaction, and resources.
Sharing (Share)	6	This risk response enlists the support of a third party to take advantage of the opportunities presented by a positive risk event. You partner with a third party, and both share in the benefits.
Sponsor	2	Individual who approves the project and provides necessary funding.
Stakeholder	1	Any individual or organization with an interest in the project. Stakeholders are both internal and external.
Stakeholder Management Plan	9	A plan that lists key stakeholder, shows their current commitment level, the desired commitment level, and outlines strategies to either sustain current commitment levels or move them.
Stakeholder Management Strategy	9	Define the strategy for managing stakeholders on your Stakeholder Register. Most common model is the power/interest model. The salience model keys on power, urgency, and legitimacy of stakeholder actions.

Term	Chapter	Definition
Stakeholder Register	3, 9	Includes key information about stakeholders. Normally includes: Identification information, Assessment Information, and Classification
Standard Deviation	5	A statistical measure of distance from a calculated mean. Risk increases as the Standard Deviation number increases.
Storming	9	Second step in the Tuckman Model. Team must overcome individual focus and issues before they can focus on project work. Leader strategy is to sell.
Strategies for Negative Risks or Threats	6	Responses to deal with negative risks. Includes Avoid, Transfer, Mitigate, and Accept.
Strategies for Positive Risks or Opportunities	6	Responses to deal with positive risks. Includes Exploit, Share, Enhance, and Accept.
Supporting	9	Provide assistance and support as needed to achieve project goals.
Supportive	9	Level of Commitment designator. Stakeholder agrees with the project.
SWOT	3	Analyze opportunities and threats based on strengths and weaknesses.
System Dynamics	5	A methodology and mathematical modeling technique to frame, understand, and discuss complex issues and problems.
Team Building	9	Help individuals bound by common purpose work with each other and independently.
Teaming Agreement	6	An informal or formal working agreement between a buyer and seller. These agreements are quite common between established sellers and buyers who share a long-term relationship.

Term	Chapter	Definition
Technical Performance Measurement	7	Tool and technique that determines if the actual technical performance achieved matches planned technical performance schedules.
Three Needs Theory	9	*See* Achievement Motivation Theory.
Three Point Estimating	5	A method of estimating that calculates the best estimate based on Pessimistic, Most Likely, and Optimistic estimates.
Time and Material	8	Contract type that is short in duration and generally used for services.
Top Down Estimating	9	*See* Analogous.
Tornado Diagram	5	Generally the result of sensitivity analysis. A tornado diagram shows a single factor such as Net Present Value (NPV). It then visually displays variables that can impact the single variable.
Transference (Transfer)	6	Risk response that transfers accountability and responsibility of a risk to a third party. The third party actually performs the work or takes accountability. There is normally a cost incurred.
Triangular Distribution	5	Probability peaks at the mean. There is a fast decrease in probability as you look at results away from the mean.
Trigger	6, 7	An early warning sign that a risk is about to occur. Initiates a contingent response strategy.
Trust Building	9	Help people to develop mutual respect, openness, understanding, and empathy, to develop communication and teamwork.
Tuckman Model	9	Five-step model that depicts growth of a team. Steps include Forming, Storming, Norming, Performing, and Adjourning.
Unaware	9	Level of Commitment designator. Stakeholder is unaware of the project.

Term	Chapter	Definition
Uniform Distribution	5	Risk is normally uniform in the early design stages of a project. Distribution becomes non-uniform in the later stages.
Unknown Risks	1, 7	Risks that have yet to be identified. A goal of solid risk management is to try to identify all Unknown Risks before they identify you!
Unknown Unknowns	7	Same as Unknown Risks.
Urgent List	4, 6	Risks requiring an immediate response.
Variance and Trend Analysis	7	Observing planned versus actual results and taking corrective action as required. A key Control Risks tool and technique.
Visualization	5	Any technique for creating images, diagrams, or animations to communicate a message.
Watch List	4, 7	Risks that you do not need to develop responses for because of a low Risk Score.
What If Scenario Analysis	5	*See* Sensitivity Analysis.
Work Breakdown Structure (WBS)	9	Output of Create Work Breakdown Structure. WBS defines activities at summary, control account, or work package levels. WBS also defines nature of project as first of its kind or recurring.
Work Breakdown Structure Dictionary	9	Part of the Scope Baseline. Provides attributes of an individual work package.
Work Performance Data (WPD)	7	Raw data generated from all Project Executing Process Group processes. Work Performance Data is reviewed, analyzed, and transformed into more useable Work Performance Information.

Term	Chapter	Definition
Work Performance Information (WPI)	7	An output of all Monitor and Control processes. WPI is an output of the Control Risks process. WPI collects pertinent WPD, and converts it into more useable information that can be used to feed the overall project Work Performance Report.
Work Performance Reports (WPR)	7	Consolidate all WPI generated from multiple Monitor and Control processes and puts it into a comprehensive project status report that covers all aspects of the project.
Workaround	7	A response to an unplanned or unknown risk.

CPSIA information can be obtained
at www.ICGtesting.com
Printed in the USA
LVOW09s2255090518
576670LV00001B/9/P